The Angel Overlords

Magickal Energy States for Manifestation

Ben Woodcroft

Copyright © 2019 by Ben Woodcroft

All rights reserved.

Published worldwide by The Power of Magick Publishing, London, England.

The publisher and author have provided this book for personal use only. You are not permitted to make the book publicly available in any way. Infringement of copyright is against the law. All images within are subject to copyright.

The author and the publisher assume no responsibility for your actions should you choose to use the ideas presented in this book.

Ben Woodcroft does not provide medical advice or suggest any techniques or methods that can be used for the treatment of medical conditions, whether physical, psychological or emotional, directly, indirectly or through implication. The author intends to share information that is general and speculative in nature, and no medical, psychological or emotional claims are made or intended. If you choose to use the information in this book, the author can accept no responsibility for your actions.

TABLE of CONTENTS

The Angel Energy States	7
The Structure of Magick	11
Choosing an Energy State	17
Exploring the Magick	23
The Workings of Effect	27
The Overlord Ritual	31
1. The Angel Ademariel	38
2. The Angel Damemiah	40
3. The Angel Rahnahdiel	42
4. The Angel Sepeshmiah	44
5. The Angel Kahdemriah	46
6. The Angel Pomariel	48
7. The Angel Iahshadiah	50
8. The Angel Alimiel	52
9. The Angel Arneniel	54
10. The Angel Kawzibiah	56
11. The Angel Dahkeriah	58
12. The Angel Iahemiel	60
13. The Angel Gahbeliah	62
14. The Angel Rahdahdiel	64
15. The Angel Kemashiel	66
16. The Angel Hahdarmiel	68
17. The Angel Rabeniel	70
18. The Angel Pedahiel	72
19. The Angel Goramiah	74
20. The Angel Ashenviel	76
21. The Angel Periviel	78
22. The Angel Abremviah	80
23. The Angel Adashniah	82
24. The Angel Hodahdiah	84
25. The Angel Televemiel	86

26. The Angel Ikapetiah	88
27. The Angel Marenshiel	90
28. The Angel Napemiah	92
29. The Angel Aremotiel	94
30. The Angel Radekiel	96
31. The Angel Temarkiel	98
32. The Angel Aledekiel	100
33. The Angel Kenoriah	102
34. The Angel Arkapiah	104
35. The Angel Marmahshiel	106
36. The Angel Sekeshiah	108
The Discovery of Magick	111
Pronouncing the Names	123
How Magick is Shared	127

The Angel Energy States

The Angel Overlords can generate an energy state within you that attracts what you want and repels what you don't want. It is a pure form of magick that works quickly and safely.

You can summon energies that will affect significant situations in your life, unlock problems that appear to be frozen, and empower your ability to manifest.

Whether you seek progress, healing, material growth, spiritual exploration, or problem-solving, these energy states are a remarkably powerful way to get what you want.

It is an established truth in occultism that you can ask angels (and other spirits) to bring you what you want, and if you do that in the right way, it can work. I've written about that kind of magick before. What you get in *this* book is different, and works by creating a state within you that gives you the power to shape your destiny.

There are thirty-six Angel Overlords, each contributing a distinctive quality that brings about an energy state which has many applications. This is not a book with a list of spells or powers, but you can trust that any situation you want to change can be changed. It can be shifted by a transformation of your energy state.

Other authors, researchers, and occultists have called the Angel Overlords by a multitude of names. They are listed as angelic princes or spirit intelligences, and other similar titles. Such labels are used liberally in other areas of occultism, but I believe it is important to allocate the Angel Overlords a title of their own. I am not the only author to do this, but I believe this is the first time the Angel Overlords have been revealed as a collective in a modern grimoire.

These angels do not sit at the top of the angelic hierarchy, but they have the authority to guide many other angels and forces that relate to these energy states. They are lords of this power and rule how it can be summoned and distributed. This is why they are known as Overlords. Despite their ability to combine other angelic powers, they are easy to summon. You work with them by using a ritual that employs a Celestial Sigil and an easy form of directed thought.

To illustrate, the angel Ademariel can bring you The Quality of Success, and will blend the power of many angels (and archangels) to produce an energy state that feels like success. With this energy inside you, becoming a part of you, it is possible to attract the people and situations you need for success. You can find the strength to manifest desires, repel doubts, and solve problems. The magick takes away the struggle and helps you to discover the opportunities that await you. This is the briefest summary of how the energy can work. If you are seeking success or any other state of being, there are numerous ways an energy state can be employed.

Instead of casting a hundred spells and performing a whole slate of rituals, you create the energy state with ease and guide your attention to the change you require. What you need then becomes real.

If there's somebody in your life that you don't want, you induce an energy that makes that person move out of your life. If you seek more money, you create an energy state that attracts the conditions and situations that make higher income possible. If you want to remove loneliness, you create energy states that repel the conditions of loneliness, while attracting the joy that makes social contact possible.

This is not passive magick or wishful thinking, but it does work in a way that feels different to magick you may be familiar with. In most magickal systems, you request a result and make room for that result. Here, you create an internal state that is then directed at the result. When there is a storm, you calm the seas; you usher in fair weather rather than battling the storm. It might not sound as dramatic as hurling thunderbolt curses or casting wealth spells, but the results should speak for themselves.

An energy state is granted to you by the angels and then focused on a problem or desire. It can be a groundbreaking way to obtain what you need and want.

If you have never worked with magick, this might sound improbable, but you can reach beyond doubt. In buying this book, you have taken the first step towards a result, and personal proof is all you need. If you choose to try this magick, you will find it is an excellent way to experience the influence that angels can have on your immediate reality.

If you *have* already experienced the benefits of a magickal result in your life, I expect this magickal technology will sound plausible. You may sense how it feels right that the angels can work in this way, bringing about a state within you that gives you the power to trigger and sustain new realities.

The magick revealed in these pages works by itself, and you don't need to buy or use anything else. If you do use other forms of magick, however, you will find these energy states can be the key to unlocking the power in all your rituals. This is a standalone text of magickal rituals that bring you what you want, but I know that many of you already work with magick, and if you do, you will probably see the potential for empowering other rituals. If a ritual is stuck, the energies you find in this book could release its potential.

If you are setting out on your magickal journey, you may find this work will one day lead you to other forms of magick, or you may find this magick is all you need. The energy states give you the broad strokes of power that shape destiny, and the precise focus of influence for reality manipulation.

You won't find the Angel Overlords or the Divine Names listed in most mainstream angel encyclopedias, although you will find some references in older grimoires and more academic texts. Some of the angel names are found in a small number of modern grimoires. If you wish to understand the origins of The Angel Overlords, I've provided additional details at the end of the book. I will also join the contemporary chorus that insists that a moment of angelic experience, or a single magickal result, teaches more than a thousand books of angelic theory. The additional material is provided only to bring confidence where there may be doubt.

I expect you may encounter word of these angels if you work extensively in occultism, but they are usually presented in a more limited or incomplete way. As far as I know, this is the first time the Angel Overlords have been revealed in a book that includes the practical magick required to employ their powers. This is the first public revelation of the Celestial Sigils and Divine Name combinations required to work with the angels directly.

Manipulating an energy state to attract a result or repel an unwanted condition, is a form of magick that will feel new and familiar, strange, yet comfortable, but most of all, effective.

Magick works in many ways, often unexpectedly and with great simplicity, surprising you with a strange coincidence or a chain of synchronicities that take you where you want to be. Take the time to know what you want, commit to getting that result, and allow the magick to work its way into strengthening your efforts to create a better life. I know of no better way to do that than by creating the energy state within you. And I know of no better way to create the energy state than to ask for it to be granted by an angel.

The Structure of Magick

The Overlords are not like any other angels. Despite their title, they don't rule over the other angels but rule over the *powers* of other angels.

The subject of angelic ranking is one that occultists have spent a great deal of time pondering, and many lengthy books are comprised of nothing more than a system of ranking. There is rarely much consistency between authors and sources, and knowing an objective truth about such rankings could be considered problematic.

For practical magick, you are able to access the powers of The Angel Overlords, and their power is the ability to create an energetic state that will repel the unwanted and attract the desired.

To gain some understanding of how this works, we'll look at just one angel from this book. That angel is Ademariel.

Ademariel is called with the Divine Names Vehu and Dameb. These Divine Names are most strongly associated with the angels Vehuel (sometimes spelled as Vehuiah), and Damebel (sometimes spelled as Damebiah.)

Vehuel and Damebel belong to a rank of angels known as the seventy-two angels of the Shemhamphoras. They are also known as 'Shem angels' and are explored in my book *Angelic Sigils, Seals and Calls*.

Associated with these Shem angels are Azriel and Demartiel, who are sometimes called Angelic Princes, Angels of Prominence, and many other titles. (Please note that Azriel is not to be confused with Azrael.)

Additional angels that provide assistance to the two Shem angels are Vavliel, Hoel, Venael, Dodniel, Mashfidael, and Bivael. Beneath these, many other angels, angelical powers, and angelic intelligences are overseen by the angels in a web of magickal power and cooperation. In all cases, the power of one or more archangels helps to oversee the connections

I could go on, showing additional connections, but you can now see that these angels work with the assistance of many other ranks of angels.

It has even been said that when the Divine Names are used alone, without calling angels, the angels are called anyway, whether you know it or not. This is a matter of speculation but indicates that a rich level of integration is important for successful magick.

Here, the various combinations of Divine Names provide you with access to thirty-six Angelic Overlords, who are able to draw power from *all* their associated angels.

When you use the Divine Names Vehu and Dameb to call Ademariel, the angel Ademariel is able to call on the power of all the angels you see listed above, as well as many, many others from ranks and orders that are too numerous to be listed.

That is true for every angel in this book. Although you work with thirty-six angels, each angel is able to draw on the wisdom and power of more angels than you can imagine.

In most magick, Divine Names are used as sparks of creative power, but here they are used as Admitting Words. By combining these specific Name pairs, you are permitted and empowered to call on the Angel Overlords.

The ritual you use to achieve this is not altogether different from rituals that are commonly known. I am not attempting to flatter your curiosity with intriguing new techniques but to provide you with magick that works.

One notable difference between this and many other books, however, is that the Celestial Sigils used do not contain Hebrew. They are written in one of the widely used Celestial Alphabets, of which there are many. They are an encoded script that has been found to work in angelic magick.

The Celestial Sigils are a visual connection to the Divine Names and the angels. In many forms of magick, Hebrew is considered to be a key to unlocking desired effects. The letters themselves are considered magickal. While this is often true, The Angel Overlords are summoned more successfully when using a Celestial Alphabet. You do not need to be able to read the letters because casting your eyes over the sigil will create the initial conditions required to raise the energy of the ritual. This is an illustration of how a Celestial Sigil is constructed:

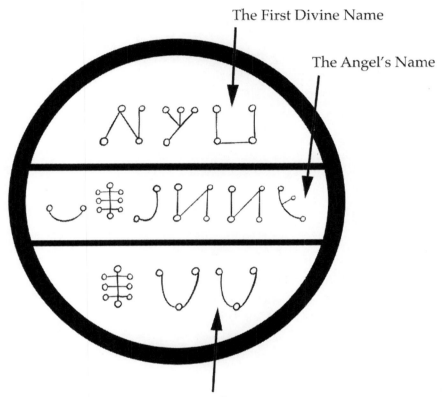

The Divine Names are placed in the upper and lower sections, with the angel's Name written across the centre. These Names could be read from right to left, as with Hebrew, but you do not need to read them. The process of gazing over the circle works, and I mention the reading direction only out of interest.

At the end of the book, there's more background information to help you understand the origins and development of angel magick. If you ever followed The Power of Magick website, you might have read early versions of that material, but the posts were only seen by about a hundred readers. I thought it fair to put them in a book like this instead, so they'll be read and understood by the people who matter. This is where such information belongs; with occultists who *use* magick, not just people who are browsing.

Those later details should be interesting, but like all background material, it's not overly important. In practice, you only need to use the instructions I'll give you, and then these angels will bring you results.

The magick ritual described later is no more complicated than other magick, but first, you must think deeply about what you want to attract, or what you wish to repel. With that decision made, the power of the angels can be brought to summon the appropriate energy. Combined with your ordinary efforts, and the beautiful machinery of synchronicity, events will begin to occur the way you want them to occur.

One of the strengths of this magick is that you often obtain substantial benefits before you get the final result you are seeking. The energy state itself is something you can feel straight away, or within hours. If you are seeking peace from an ongoing struggle with an enemy, the energy state of peace will come to you, and you will feel the peace, and that means you are relieved of the problem before the problem itself is cured. This is tremendously empowering, because feeling that state of completion then enables the actual result to manifest more readily.

The magick doesn't always work this way, however, and sometimes you may induce the energy without feeling it, but this needn't be frustrating. It takes trust and patience, but if you accept that the process of performing the magick summons the energy, and know that the energy is within you, that will enable your result to come about.

Often, the energy will be felt at once, especially if you are sensitive or open-minded, open-hearted, or willing to change, and that can be wonderful. If you feel nothing, do not despair, but trust that the magick is within you, and then observe as matters begin to change appropriately.

If you work with this magick, you will discover that by building a succession of results, the transformation that occurs over months and years can be almost miraculous. Some people report immediate results when working with angels, and although you can allow for this possibility, do not rely on magick to work this way. Understand the guidance I provide in the next chapter. If you can do that, I believe that the changes will come. Some will be rapid, some may be instantaneous, but many will be subtle, gentle, taking time to be noticeable, and they can be much more powerful for being so.

Choosing an Energy State

You can use this magick when you have an urgent need, or when you are building steadily to a desired result or a changed state of existence. Choosing which magick to use requires some effort on your part so that you use the most appropriate magick for your needs.

In an era when there are so many books offering lists of rituals for every problem you might face, I believe some people are losing the ability to notice where they are in life, and what they need. Faced with any challenge, they reach for the first ritual or spell they can find, wasting powerful magick on minor problems, or using the wrong magick for their situation. This rush to perform magick can lead to weaker results. Somebody who tosses curses around might not get as much satisfaction from life as somebody who deals with the underlying issues and finds peace.

The answer to this is the simplest solution imaginable, and because it is so simple, it is one of the most overlooked steps in magick. And that is, you should decide what it is that you really want to achieve. Better still, determine what it is you want to feel. Think about that, and you know where you are going.

It won't be as ephemeral as, 'I want to be happy.' But if you think about any facet of your life, from your finances to your relationships, you should find that you almost immediately know how you would like to feel, compared to how you feel now. And as you contemplate, your dreams may become bigger, and you will get a clearer picture of what you want, how good it could be, and how that would make you feel. This isn't wishing, hoping, or positive thinking. It is the beginning of your magickal work.

Magick begins when you start to think about what you want to achieve *with* magick. The process of thinking about, and believing in the power of magick to affect the world is not an ordinary way of thinking. It may come to feel quite ordinary, but it is very far from the way most people spend their lives. An ordinary person will think, worry, plan, guess, and hope their way through a day, week, or year, but they will not spend a single moment thinking about performing a magick ritual to change reality. Most people will never go into a state of mind where they believe that performing magick will bring a magickal result.

It sounds like nothing, but it is an important part of magick, rarely talked about because it happens almost automatically. You buy a magick book, and you look through to find what ritual might work for you, and in doing that you have begun the magick because you have moved into that state of being where your thoughts are aligned with the belief that magick brings results.

The reason I am talking about this process here is that it is vital for you to spend some time thinking about how the magick could work for you, and what result you want. This is not idle time. Such time is never wasted, and it *is* an act of magick.

By choosing to think about your problems and desires, and the magick that could work with them, you are reaching within to imprint your desire on the future. Before you even begin the magick, your magick has begun.

This doesn't mean you need to work out every detail and define the exact way that result will manifest, and such an approach would be counter-productive. It means only that you should be guided by whatever it is that preoccupies you, whatever situation prods your consciousness, and whatever problem is impeding your progress.

It might sound obvious to say 'use magick for the things you want,' but many people do not take the time to settle into their awareness of the feelings of the present moment, to know what it is they want to change.

People often say that if they could earn some more money, they would be happy. I know they are wrong, in most cases. There is magick in this book to help attract more money, but is that what you really need? Perhaps, but perhaps not. If you are unable to enjoy life because poverty or debt are getting in the way, then you do need money, and you *should* work on money first, or early in your quest. But in many cases, people seek money because they think it will be like a painkiller for the other problems faced. Money rarely helps as much as you believe or hope.

Does this matter? Do you have to use the magick most appropriate for your needs? You are free to use any magick you like, at any time, but I have observed that results will be more highly charged and most rewarding when you spend some time deciding what it is that you genuinely want.

This is not an excuse for procrastination. A ritual performed today or tomorrow, after ten minutes of contemplation, is far more useful to you than a ritual that comes after a month of wondering or deliberating about what will be best for you.

When you want to use magick, think about the problem or situation you are in, and then look at the feelings it generates. Does this give you any clues about what you might need to change, what you want to attract, or what you want to repel?

If you're feeling the need for more money, consider the feelings that you have about money at this very moment, and you may find that other ideas come to the surface. You may realise that you are, in truth, frustrated with somebody you are working with. Or you may realise there is a problem in a relationship that's making you focus on money too much. Or it may be that you realise a lack of money *is* affecting you and making you feel disempowered. Whatever you discover, you should then spend more time contemplating the magick that might work best to bring a solution.

More than half the time, your first guess will be right. You think you want more money, and you really do. But I still believe it is worth spending ten minutes or more, to think over the issues and look at your feelings. It will pay off when you come to choose which angel to work with. And if, after ten minutes or so, you think exactly the same as you did before you started, you have not wasted any time. It is the process of looking within that sets this in motion for you.

It's not all that different from finding yourself daydreaming about what you want. It's even quite close to the feeling of worrying about a problem and wishing there was a solution. In ordinary life, it is an ordinary process. You feel pain that something is not right, and you want to feel something else. When magick is your intention, that simple act of choosing the new feeling that you want becomes a highly magickal process.

I am not encouraging you to visualise your future to make it come true. You are only using this exploration of feelings to discover what it is that you want to feel in the future, to help you choose the correct energy state, and thus the correct angel, to obtain your desired future.

Choosing an angel, in some books, can be as easy as looking through a table which shows you which angels work for money, which work for love, which for success, but that will not be the case here. The energy states come from the qualities that are conveyed by the angel and cannot be summarised too briefly, or at too much length. I have provided you with the outlines that I have used to work with these angels. There is enough information for you to understand each energy state, each angel's qualities, and the potential this has for practical magick. But there is not too *much* information. If I told you every experience that's been reported with these angels, you would be left without the room to imagine. Speculation, daydreaming, and wondering all help you obtain an intuition about what an angel can do for you. That intuition is something that should not be overlooked.

That means you will need to read through the book, and read about each angel's powers to see what's appropriate for you now. When you come to look through the angels' powers, think of it not as reading, but as a magickal act where you are letting your inner self reach out to the angels, and in turn, they may respond by sparking your intuition.

Do you need to meditate, set some time aside, or just think about this while you're driving home from work? This is a personal matter. I have found that sitting quietly and contemplating my feelings is more effective than something too casual. It helps to be quiet, alone, and with time to examine how you feel. Although this somewhat lengthy chapter may seem to have done nothing but repeat a single point, if you read it again you may find that it does more, and encourages self-exploration while stating and restating this important point.

The descriptions of the powers are only a starting point, to urge your imagination and dreams into action. The descriptions have been written to give enough information to define the powers, without limiting their potential. For example, although there is no power listed 'to increase income' for Ademariel, your understanding of the powers should make it clear that if you want to increase your income, the energy of success could do that. If something feels like success to you, then the energy will work to bring that success. I will not go into further detail because it is important that you allow your intuition to guide you. Don't be limited by the descriptions, but let yourself be inspired. And remember that if it feels right to you, it *is* right and it will work.

Exploring the Magick

To better illustrate how this magick works, I'll walk you through an example. Although magick books typically explain all the details and all the things you need to know before giving an example, I'm going to do it the other way around. I think, in this case, knowing the bigger picture of how a ritual can work, will make everything else make more sense as you read the finer details.

For this example, we shall imagine that six months ago you opened a café in a niche part of town, with a menu and style that should appeal to locals. Your efforts have paid off, but only just, and your business is not doing as well as you want. You spend time reading through the descriptions of the angels, and when you are familiar with the energy states, you spend an hour thinking about what needs to change.

After this contemplation, you are quite convinced that it would be most helpful to summon The Quality of Success, bestowed by the first angel in the book, Ademariel. You like the fact that the energy state will repel situations and obstacles that relate to your doubts and fears. You also like that the energy can give you the strength to become successful while feeling pleasure in all that you receive. Your plan is to direct the energy of the ritual at your business, to bring a boost in success.

When planning your ritual, you will often note lots of potential side benefits, as listed above, but you will still choose one main area where you wish to direct the energy of the ritual. It may be quite specific, such as an increase in customers, or an increase in the amount customers spend, or perhaps even an improvement in reputation. Or it can be more general. In this example, you have chosen to leave it quite general, directing the energy to bring a boost of success to your business.

When contemplating this, you feel that your business is not doing as well as it could, and you can imagine how good it would feel to get a general boost. If things go better, and you can look back and say, 'Yes, my business definitely received a boost that month,' you know how good that will feel. With that all in mind, you are ready to perform the ritual.

Before you begin the ritual, you take some time to look at the words below the Celestial Sigil. For the angel Ademariel, they are Vehu, Dameb, Ademariel, and the sound OO. For each angel, you will see this same pattern. The first two words are the Divine Names, then the angel's Name is listed, and finally, there is a sound, such as OO, OH, AH, or EYE, which you will chant during the ritual.

Next to each Name, you will see a phonetic guide, showing you how to say the Name. For Vehu it is VEH-WHO. For Dameb it is DAM-EBB. For Ademariel it is ADD-EM-AH-REE-ELL. You can take some time to become familiar with the Names, learning to say them effortlessly. You do not need to pronounce the Names perfectly because the sigil will guide the correct angel to become present, but you need to feel confident when you say the words. If you need further guidance on pronunciation, there's an additional chapter covering this at the end of the book.

You then find a time to perform the ritual. We'll imagine that just after sunset you work in your bedroom, undisturbed but with the curtains open so there is sufficient twilight to read. You have written a summary of the ritual in note form, and you have the book open to reveal the angel's Celestial Sigil, and the Names you will speak. (If you are using a device, and if the required Names and words don't all fit on your screen, you may write them in your notebook as well.)

You perform the ritual, as instructed in the upcoming chapter called The Overlord Ritual. In summary, this is how you perform the ritual. You chant a word that connects you to Universal Power, and then gaze at the sigil. You then speak the two Divine Names. When you have done that you speak the Name of the angel. You then chant a sound, while contemplating the energy state and how it can resolve your problem, and you allow yourself to feel the energy state arise within you. You have no expectations, but you chant the sound for a minute or so, noting and enjoying feelings that arise. You might feel a sense of power and success, happiness, gratitude, or something less easy to label. You may even feel a warm or comforting energy within you. In some cases, you won't feel much at all, but you don't let this concern you, and after a few minutes, you close the ritual as instructed.

In the days that follow you know that waiting for the magick to work is counterproductive, and so you focus your efforts on doing the best you can to improve your business. You do this with a sense of ease and expectation that all will be well, but without looking for proof, evidence, or indications that the magick is working. During the first ten days, you may feel the energy of success within you, quite strongly. You may notice that there are fewer problems and that things begin to turn around. Although you are not looking for results, you feel grateful that some things are definitely changing. After several weeks have passed, you look back and know that, without doubt, there was a great boost to your business in the previous weeks, and you are now in a better position to build your business further.

This is one basic example, and there are several other ways to use the magick. You may, for example, use several rituals (with a single angel) to affect different aspects of a situation over a longer period of time.

I will expand on this first example by looking at what would happen if the results weren't quite what you expected. You have performed the ritual, and you've done what you can, but when you look back after several weeks, you feel that something is preventing your business from flourishing. You can feel that the energy of success was working to make things better, but there was resistance. You realise, after thinking about it some more, that you have some fear of success and guilt about making too much money. This is a bohemian part of town, and you're worried that if you do too well or become too popular, you'll lose the respect of your customers. Although this fear is unfounded, it's holding you back. You choose to work with Rahnahdiel to generate The Quality of

Receiving. You direct the energy at your guilty feelings about money, and you find in the coming weeks that everything improves. By healing this underlying issue, you make success something you are willing to receive. You then choose to invoke The Quality of Success once more, knowing that there will be less resistance this time.

In most cases, you perform one ritual and get a result, and there is no need to look for underlying problems. But if you find a situation refuses to change, even though it should be within reach, you may want to look at potential issues that lie beneath the surface. Coming at a problem in this way can be the key to beginning change.

You will notice the emphasis I have placed on working towards reasonable change. You are not trying to become the best and most successful business owner in the country during the next week. You are taking things slowly and steadily, without desperately waiting for results. Magick can bring great change, and if you need great change urgently you can seek it, but the most consistent results come when you push your personal reality in small stages.

You do not have to force belief or convince yourself that magick will work. You can forget about the magick until something good happens that makes you notice the result. When something good happens, always notice it and feel pleased that the magick has worked. You may not feel the energy state at all, but if you do, you can also enjoy that. Don't seek it, yearn for it, or focus on it. Enjoy it if it's there, but put your main focus on your effort to bring change in the world. When you can do that, the energy within you flows out, and the magick of that energy brings the changes you desire.

The Workings of Effect

Before working with magick, there are some details that may assist you, and some common questions I would like to answer.

You do not need to make any sacrifice or offering, and there is no need to summon the angels to give thanks. You don't need to concern yourself with so-called backlash. There is a great deal of superstition that warns you never to use magick without making a payment, or you'll be punished by 'bad karma.' If you believe this, I have no way of convincing you otherwise, but my knowledge of magick tells me that we have the right to make choices. This does not mean there are no consequences (because with all change comes the need for your response and ability to live with the change), but there is never any punishment for getting more than you deserve. If you are afraid of magick, start with something small and generous that may help others as well as yourself, or share the benefits of the magick with others when they are received, until your fear of magick subsides.

You should also know the intended and expected duration of the magick. Occultists are often asked how long a ritual 'lasts for', and there is rarely an adequate answer. Sometimes the magickal effect lasts until the result is achieved, and at other times it can bring a change that is permanent. It can even be argued that all magick is permanent because any change, no matter how small, has changed the course of your life. But the question is asked because people want to know how often to repeat the magick and how often they can do new rituals. In this case, with the energy state invoked by the Angel Overlord, the answer is easier than usual. The energy state lasts for about ten days.

This is not an exact science, and you may feel the energy subside before then, or it may last a while longer. It's also important to know this doesn't mean you always get your result on day ten. You may get a result immediately, or it may be that the events that are set in motion during those ten days bring a result to you many weeks from now.

To understand this, you need to remember that the magick of the Angel Overlords works on two levels. The energy works on the goal or result you are aiming for, but it also affects you more generally by generating that energy state within you. In the most basic terms, if you perform magick to bring more passion to a relationship, that goal may be reached some weeks from now, but you may feel more passion for life, friends, and other aspects of your life, during the ten days that follow the ritual.

It has already been implied that when you perform the magick, you may experience the benefits of the quality you have invoked before you even get your results. In some cases, this enables the result to come about more easily. The quality you experience paves the way for the result you seek.

If, for example, you have used the magick of Kahdemriah to reduce misunderstanding in a relationship, that is your goal, the result you seek, and it may occur immediately or some time from now. But the magick also works to create an energy state known as The Quality of Relating, and in this state, you will feel clarity, peace, and ease in problematic relationships. The experience of the quality will last for about ten days and may have many benefits in several areas of your life. It will also make you more open to receiving the result you have aimed for because you are already residing in the aligned energy state. The energy state will remain activated within you for approximately ten days. (If you get your result before then, the magick keeps working, which can ensure the result is locked into reality.)

In practice, this means that if you sense the energy state and gain benefit from its effects, you will do so for approximately ten days. If you do not feel the energy state directly, it will still be affecting you and your reality on a subconscious level for approximately ten days. In terms of the result, it means that the work of the magick takes place during those ten days, planting the seed of the new reality. That reality may sprout, bloom, and blossom in moments, or the growth may be slow. Although the ten-day period is accurate when describing the immediate and noticeable energy of the ritual, the result should not be expected to come in ten days. It may take longer.

If you want to repeat the ritual after ten days, you can, but often, you don't need to, and it can be more effective to assume the result will come eventually.

There is another way of working, where you work with a single angel on several related issues. Using the example from the previous chapter, you may decide that as well as seeking a general boost to the business, you will also perform three more rituals with Ademariel. One ritual could be used to attract the right people who can help your business. Another ritual could be used to reduce the feelings of struggle. And you could complete this with a ritual to increase income.

It is possible to perform one ritual each day so that after four days, everything is in place. A more patient approach can be interesting, where you allow three or four days to pass (or even many more,) before you perform the next ritual. You could even space the rituals out by ten days, so that you are invoking The Quality of Success for forty days, with each result building on the strength of the others. How you use the magick is up to you.

Each ritual only needs to be performed once, and you should not repeat a ritual to enhance or improve the energy. Although this might seem like a good idea, it creates a subconscious feeling of failure, as though you believe the magick is not strong enough. Instead, let go of the magick and assume it will work. You can, however, repeat the ritual every ten days or so, if you are seeking sustained improvements in the same area. With the example we gave, you might perform the same ritual every ten days, or perhaps every month, to allow the quality of success to improve your business continually.

Should you want to perform several rituals at once with several angels, I advise against it, and this is the main limitation of the system. Although this is powerful magick, it does not work as well when you try to generate several energy states at once. That means that if you work with one angel for months at a time, you can't work with any other angels from this book at the same time. This isn't as bad as it sounds, because in most cases, you won't work with an angel for months unless that's a massively high priority. Usually, you perform one ritual, and that's enough. Ten days later, you are free to work with any other angel on whatever situation you desire, whether or not it is related to the first one.

In a single week, you might perform four rituals with Sepeshmiah, and then ten days later you could work with Pomariel, and ten days later you could work with Alimiel. This amount of magick is acceptable. But if you were to work with all three angels at once, the energy might be reduced with the results lessened. This doesn't mean it's impossible to combine and overlap, but I never advise it, and I believe that the ideal approach is to work with one energy state at a time. After ten days have passed, you can work with another angel.

You are free to use all other forms of magick at the same time as this book, and there is no danger of the energy state cancelling out or corrupting other magick. You may notice, however, that energy states have a positive impact on other forms of magick when they are in alignment. If you are performing success magick from another book and generating the energy of success with this book, you may find the other magick improves greatly. This does not mean you need to buy another book and use other forms of magick. It does mean that if you are using other forms of magick, you now understand how you can enhance the overall energy of your occult workings.

To begin, I suggest taking it slowly. Try one ritual, with one angel, give it time to work, and enjoy the changes that occur.

The Overlord Ritual

If you have read my book *Angelic Sigils, Seals and Calls* you will be familiar with some aspects of this process. Please note that the ritual is not the same, and the differences are important. Follow the instructions for this ritual when working with these angels.

The preparation mentioned earlier, in which you spend time knowing what it is you feel and what you want to feel, should have equipped you for the ritual. There is no need for complex purification that is sometimes found in some magickal systems. If you have worked with my book, *Angelic Protection Magick*, you will see there is a sequence of three rituals that can be performed before a ritual. You are free to do so when working with the Angel Overlords, but please do not feel this is a requirement. If you are sincere in your intention, you are ready to use this magick.

The Angel Overlords respond most readily when you know yourself. When you invite the angel to be in your presence through this ritual, it will respond if you have understood your own wants and needs.

You can perform your rituals on any day of the week and during any phase of the moon. If you prefer to time your magick to astrological phases you are welcome to, but it is not required for results.

During the ritual, you will look at the Celestial Sigil, and you will speak words, names, and sounds. Your voice is a magickal tool. Although speech may seem ordinary, it is not. We have the power to express emotions, make commands, and cause all manner of things to happen with our voice. By shaping the very breath of life into vibrations, we create sounds that communicate intention. In magick, these vibrations are sufficient to complete an angelic connection. Your voice becomes an echo of your soul, shaped by your personality and your desires, and when speaking the simple sounds of this ritual, your voice gives the angels an awareness of you and what you need.

Set some time aside where you can be alone to focus on the ritual with ease. You should aim to experience the magick rather than spit the words out as fast as you can. The more magickal it feels, the better the results will be. Remember the scope of what you are involved with and allow yourself to feel some awe. You are not casting a spell but contacting angels. It should not be overwhelming, but nor should it feel trivial.

I prefer to work after sunset, in a room illuminated by a single candle or by twilight. You may prefer to work at dawn or any other time of day that feels right to you. If you can only perform a ritual in fifteen stolen minutes, while everybody is out of the house, that is also going to work, but try to make it feel special and sacred, and remember the enormity of what you are attempting.

When you have found a time and place to perform the ritual without disturbance or distraction, you may sit, kneel, stand or even lie down, but for the sake of practicality put yourself in a comfortable place where this book is clearly visible. If you have taken notes to assist with the ritual, they should be with you. (I suggest that you write a short summary of this ritual, to guide you while keeping this book open on the angel's page. In time, you may learn the ritual, and no notes will be required.)

In this example, I will assume that you are calling the thirty-sixth angel, Sekeshiah, to invoke The Quality of Abundance. You are seeking to obtain financial support for an important project, and you believe that the energy of abundance will bring you the money you need.

To begin each ritual, chant EE-AH-OH-EH three times. Chanting doesn't have to be loud or dramatic, but it has slightly more intention than merely saying the words. To chant successfully, say this word three times with the intention of opening the ritual. Let your voice feel strong and confident.

This sound, EE-AH-OH-EH, is a vocalisation of the name of God, known as the Tetragrammaton, and is often written in

English as YHWH, and sometimes spoken as Yahweh. It can even be vocalized by naming the individual Hebrew letters, as something like YUD HEH VAHV HEH. There are many variations on this, some accurate and some not so accurate. If you don't believe in God in the traditional sense, you can think of this as the name of Universal Power.

I have found that when you run the sounds of EE, AH, OH and EH together, it sounds similar to Yahweh, but not quite the same. In this book, YHWH is pronounced as EE-AH-OH-EH. This sound is also quite close to the Greek IAO (pronounced EE-AH-OH, which is a name of God that is used in many magickal traditions.)

I believe that it helps to think of these short sounds as resonances that lead to the name of God. This is more useful than thinking that God's name is actually Yahweh. There are many names of God, so consider these as a pathway to God, however you perceive God, or if you prefer, to Universal Power or Omnipotence.

You do not need to think or feel anything in particular, except that you are opening the ritual. In choosing to speak these words, you confirm your intention to work magick.

As described earlier, the Divine Names and angel Names are written in a Celestial Alphabet, contained within the Celestial Sigils. By guiding your eyes over the shapes of the 'letters' you absorb and activate the magickal connection. Your purpose is to let go of your thoughts and hopes regarding the ritual and your desired result, and merely to make contact with the angel. As such, spend about a minute letting your eyes move over the Celestial Letters in the sigil. You do not need to do this in any order or in any specific way, but let your gaze be loose, almost blurry, as though you are letting the letters in rather than staring at their details.

Keep the Celestial Sigil in view as you proceed, looking back to it most of the time. You don't need to stare, but it should remain in your awareness, even as you glance at your notes. You speak the pair of Divine Names to gain admittance to the Angel Overlord. In the case of Sekeshiah, the Divine Names are

Menad and Dani, pronounced as MEN-AHD and DAH-NEE. You only need to say these Names once each.

Know that by speaking this unique combination of Divine Names, you have now been admitted into the presence of the angel. All you need to do to complete the connection is to speak the angel's Name. In this example, it is Sekeshiah, pronounced as SEK-ESH-EE-AH. You only need to say this once, and you may immediately feel the tingle of presence and contact.

Your ability to sense an angel's presence is not important, but I have found these angels, more than any others, will make their presence felt at this point. There may be a noise, a feeling of the air softening, a chill, warmth, distant music, or just a gentle feeling that something is happening. Often, you will feel a presence, as though somebody is close by. Do not be afraid, and know that this is safe, and it was your intention. Also, do not yearn for sensation. Some people feel more than others, and if you feel nothing, you can be assured that the magick will work anyway.

Only now do you turn your attention to the problem you wish to solve, and in doing so, you summon the appropriate energy. You do not need to think of the energy state itself, and this is fortunate because trying to feel a sensation such as The Quality of Abundance is too abstract. All you need to do is think about the result you want while making the sound. In this case, the sound is OO, and you repeat it over and over, like a gentle chant, while thinking about your result. In this case, you would think about how it would feel to get the financial support for your project.

At this stage, focus on the feelings, not the mechanism. Do not waste your time asking the angel for help, or specifying how the problem should be solved. All you need to do is focus on the feeling you wish to obtain. This is as easy as daydreaming about what you want. Here, you want that feeling of excitement and relief that comes from getting financial support. Feel that. Don't worry about who will give you the support, or how. Forget those details. Instead, feel what you want to feel in the future, by daydreaming about it.

Your efforts to achieve this feeling are supported by the presence of the angel, and by chanting the sound. This can be a gentle sound, chanted at your own pace, in a way that feels comfortable to you.

To clarify, the energy state you require will be summoned by this process, without you ever having to focus on the desired energy state itself. At no point do you need to think about the energy of abundance. You may feel it, and you may sense other emotions and sensations linked to this, but you may not. Your purpose is to imagine how it would feel to get your result while chanting the sound.

I cannot stress strongly enough that you should not focus on how the problem will be solved. If you want somebody to leave your place of work because they are disruptive and arrogant, you only need to think about how great you would feel if they were gone. You don't need to imagine a sequence of events, such as them being caught for a misdemeanour and then being fired. The wisdom of *how* will be handled by the angelic energy state that resides within you, on a subconscious level.

In the real world, of course, when the ritual is over, you may need to focus on the details of how something is achieved, but during the ritual, keep it pure by focussing on how you think you will feel. If you find this difficult, don't worry. You only need to think about getting your result while making the sound. If it's something you want, the emotional response you feel, no matter how slight, will cause the energy to move within you, and then be expressed from within you.

You may feel the need to chant for five minutes or more but only do this if you *really* feel the need. In most cases, a minute is more than enough, and you can stop chanting the sound as soon as you have felt some satisfaction. If you can grasp that feeling of having the result, as though it has already happened, trust that the energy state is now within you. The angel has heard you, has been called to your presence, and will grant the energy state to you. All you need to do now is close the ritual and go about your life as normal.

To close the ritual, you again say EE-AH-OH-EH three times, but this time it is less of a chant and is almost whispered, as though you are letting the magick settle. This will help you return to normality.

After a ritual, you may sense the energy within you, often in your heart, and sometimes in your stomach. Some people feel the energy in their head, usually between the temples. It will always be a pleasant feeling. Enjoy it if it is there, but do not feel you are missing out if you feel nothing. Disappointment will imprint the magick with the wrong feeling, so just let the ritual end and continue with your day.

I will not say, 'Try not to think about the magick,' because that is guaranteed to make you think about the magick. Instead, find something else that will occupy your attention so that you don't waste energy worrying about the magick. If you keep a magick journal, you can make notes before returning to complete normality, but after that, you should try to do something quite ordinary and let the magick go.

I mentioned that I light a candle, but this is only to create a mood, and it is not required. If you cannot find the privacy to work out loud, you can imagine the words, but this is rarely as effective. It is worth taking the time to find a place where you can be undisturbed for the time it takes to perform the ritual.

You may want to write a summary of the above, in your own words, to remind you of how to perform the ritual. This is better than using a summary I could provide because it allows you to note the points that are important to you. If you are able to learn the ritual, over time, you can perform the ritual without any notes, but this is not important. If you need notes, use them.

The following pages contain all the details you need to work with The Angel Overlords. The first page describes the angel's powers. The second page contains the Celestial Sigil, the Divine Names, the Angel Name, and the sound that you chant. (EE-AH-OH-EH is used at the beginning and end of every ritual but is not shown on these pages, as that would be needless repetition.)

1. The Angel Ademariel

The Quality of Success

The Quality of Success is an energy state where you feel pleasure in your progress, gratitude for what you have received, and increased strength from your ability to manifest desires. The energy will attract people and situations that enable success to be possible.

By summoning this quality, you induce an energy that makes it easier to find the strength to become successful in any area of your life. If you are working on a project that needs a boost in success, or an initial success, this energy will attract a reality where your desires become real.

The energy state will repel situations, feelings, and obstacles related to lack, doubt about your abilities, limiting beliefs, feelings of unworthiness, the sense of struggle, or any other emotional or situational state that hinders your ability to succeed.

Ademariel

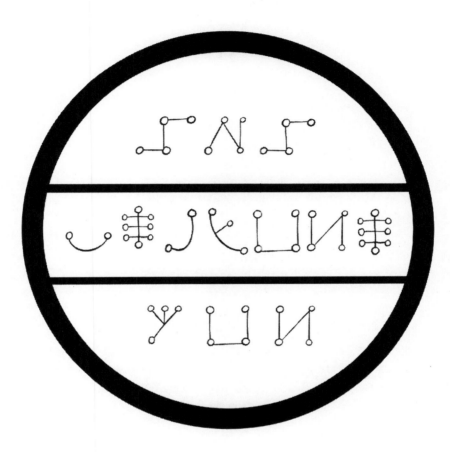

Vehu (VEH-WHO)

Dameb (DAM-EBB)

Ademariel (ADD-EM-AH-REE-ELL)

OO

2. The Angel Damemiah

The Quality of Movement

The Quality of Movement is an energy state that is a highly charged creative flow. It is a state where you feel like change is not only possible but probable and easy to achieve.

By summoning this quality, you induce an energy that enables a stuck or frozen situation to become more changeable, so that you can influence or guide that change without force.

It is the opposite of procrastination and fear, enabling you to create confidently and without hesitation. The energy enables you to move forward from a difficult situation, aiding emotional or physical recovery.

This energy is the opposite of loneliness (which is a form of stagnation). It can remove feelings of isolation and attract a stronger flow of social and emotional connections.

Damemiah

Yeli (YELL-EE)

Veval (VEH-VAHL)

Damemiah (DAH-MEM-EE-AH)

EE

3. The Angel Rahnahdiel

The Quality of Receiving

The Quality of Receiving is an energy state that removes any guilt you might feel about receiving money, love, power, success, or any other benefit.

Guilt is an energy of exclusion, so the energy state of receiving expels feelings of guilt in regards to obtaining more. Upbringing and the customs of society, amongst other things, can leave you with low receptive energy. You are not good at receiving and enjoying, because of your guilt. You may feel others deserve more, that money is evil, that having more is wrong. This energy state will help you overcome such guilt, letting you feel deep gratitude for what you have now, and what you want to come into your life. This can make all manifestation more likely, not just for material desires but also for emotional desires. Many people are unreceptive to emotional intimacy, and the quality of receiving can make it easier to allow love, intimacy, or passion into your life.

Receiving is not passive; it is an energy, a flow of power that makes way for desires to manifest, and is a way to remove internal and subconscious blockages so that you can experience joy. In any area of life where nothing seems to work, or where there is struggle, it is possible you need to become more receptive to your desire.

Rahnahdiel

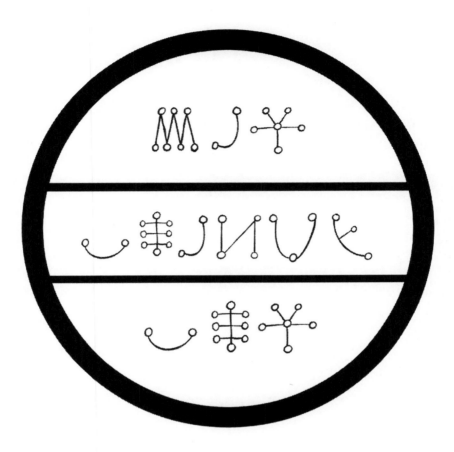

Sit (SEAT)

Sehahl (SEH-AHL)

Rahnahdiel (RAH-NAH-DEE-ELL)

OH

4. The Angel Sepeshmiah

The Quality of Soothing

The Quality of Soothing is an energy state that can ease emotional and physical pain. It helps to remove lingering bitterness, resentment, or other emotions that are damaging to your wellbeing. It is an excellent state for removing feelings of regret, or sadness over a broken relationship or the loss of a loved one.

By summoning this quality, you induce an energy that can help you feel so rejuvenated that you are better able to perceive your purpose and potential. If you are feeling stuck in life, being soothed by this energy can put you in a place where you have the inner strength and clarity to see the best way forward.

Sepeshmiah

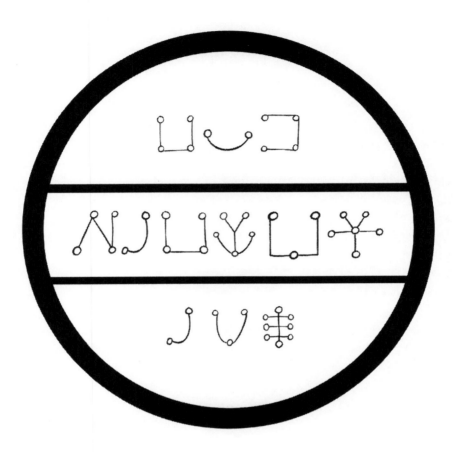

Elem (ELL-EM)

Ani (AH-NEE)

Sepeshmiah (SEP-ESH-ME-AH)

EE

5. The Angel Kahdemriah

The Quality of Relating

The Quality of Relating is an energy state that brings clarity and peace to relationships of all kinds. If any of your relationships, from romantic connections to working relationships, are suffering from troubled feelings or a lack of clarity, this energy will bring relief. The clarity and peace will be induced within you but will often have an effect on those around you as well, so that they are better able to relate to you. This can greatly reduce misunderstandings, resentments, and other problems that have lingered for some time.

By summoning this quality, you induce an energy that can ease troubled and confused emotions. It will also help you understand the reality of your feelings, helping you to see if apparent infatuations and yearnings are based on real feelings or something more trivial and temporary. If a relationship has potential, inducing this energy state can make the relationship grow stronger, more adventurous, and more confident, building trust between you. The energy works on all relationships, so expect it to have many positive effects beyond those intended, both on group and individual relationships.

Kahdemriah

Mahash (MAH-HAHSH)

Hachash (HAH-KAHSH)

Kahdemriah (KAH-DEM-REE-AH)

AH

6. The Angel Pomariel

The Quality of Harmony

The Quality of Harmony is an energy state where you feel a sense of calm mercy in your body. Emotions are experienced in many ways, but feelings of calm, mercy, forgiveness, and relief are often felt in your flesh and bones. Through the energy of harmony, you will feel this peaceful state.

By summoning this quality, you induce an energy that enables you to feel calm and peaceful, despite the attacks and negativity of others. If you wish to forgive, the energy will enable you to do that without any discomfort. If you wish to feel somebody else's forgiveness, this energy can help to attract their mercy. When you induce this energy, people are more willing to connect with you honestly and peacefully, without resentment. If you are stuck in an ongoing argument or a difficult relationship, the energy of harmony will bring peace to you, felt throughout your body, and that will be sensed by the other person, so that peace may come between you.

Pomariel

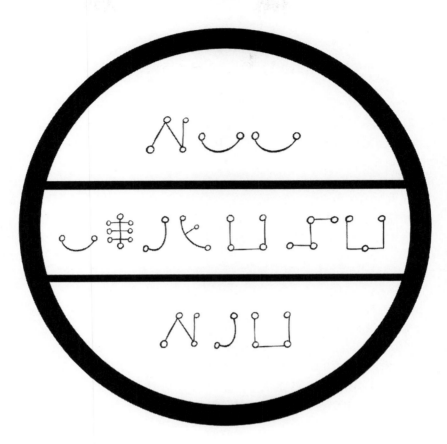

Lelah (LEH-LAH)

Mih (MEE)

Pomariel (PAW-MAH-REE-ELL)

EYE

7. The Angel Iahshadiah

The Quality of Love

The Quality of Love is an energy state that enables you to connect to the pure emotion of love without self-deception or illusion. If you are in a relationship and sense that it is developing into a loving relationship, this energy will let you feel the love at its true depth. Where infatuation and blind hope can lead you to feel more than is real, this energy will allow you to feel and express genuine love. If the love is not real, or not yet developed, you will gain an insight into what your relationship is really like, and how it may develop.

If you are already in a loving relationship, the energy can be used to eradicate or lessen old habits that prevent the full expression of love, and can enable you to feel and project the depths of the love that brought you together in the first place.

By summoning this quality, you induce an energy that will make you aware of all the loving relationships in your life, and will make you project an aura of warmth and sincerity that will be appealing to all who meet you. If somebody has doubts about you, this energy will help remove those doubts. The energy will not make everybody fall in love with you, and cannot seduce, but it will have an effect on anybody who has feelings for you. Many relationships and friendships can benefit, and a potential relationship may be urged into existence. The energy also enables you to let go of negative attachments, where you feel obliged to be around people through unwanted obligations rather than genuine love for them, bringing great freedom.

Iahshadiah

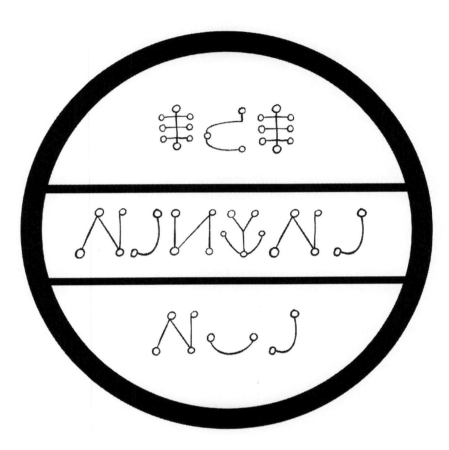

Acha (AK-AH)

Yelah (YELL-AH)

Iahshadiah (EE-AH-SHAH-DEE-AH)

EH

8. The Angel Alimiel

The Quality of Connection

The Quality of Connection is an energy state that enables you to connect with other people in a way that lets you see beyond the obvious. Whether you are focussed on a personal relationship, a work association, or your connection to a group of people, this energy will let you understand what you receive from them and what they receive from you. It will help you understand how and why you are connected, and will enable you to understand what the connection means to them. In some cases, this can act as a clear warning, when you see that your need is negative, or that other people are using you in some way. Often, though, this energy gives a more mystical insight into these connections which lets you understand the relationships, their potential, and their meaning, in a much deeper way.

By summoning this quality, you induce an energy that not only gives clarity regarding your connection to people, but also helps to remove your social fears and anxieties. It brings trust between yourself and those who are worthy of your trust, and helps remove negativity and doubts within important relationships.

Alimiel

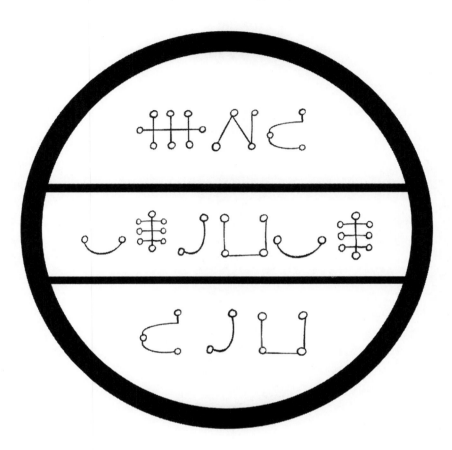

Kahet (KAH-HET)

Mich (MEEK)

Alimiel (AL-EE-ME-ELL)

OO

9. The Angel Arneniel

The Quality of Wisdom

The Quality of Wisdom is an energy state that enables you to understand what others really mean. With this knowledge you can plan for the best possible future. At any time where you feel that you need a better understanding of somebody else, this energy will draw their message within, so you understand what it is they are really trying to say. Even if they are unclear, the energy of wisdom will bring you understanding. When you are making plans that you believe require a wise appraisal of the facts, rather than emotional or intuitive decisions, this energy will bring the strength of wisdom to you.

By summoning this quality, you induce an energy that will make you wise in all matters. It will not remove your ability to be intuitive or emotional, but will balance all feelings with a shrewd understanding of the larger issues and possible futures. When making big decisions, this power is extremely useful, and can even be summoned at the same time as more intuitive powers.

Arneniel

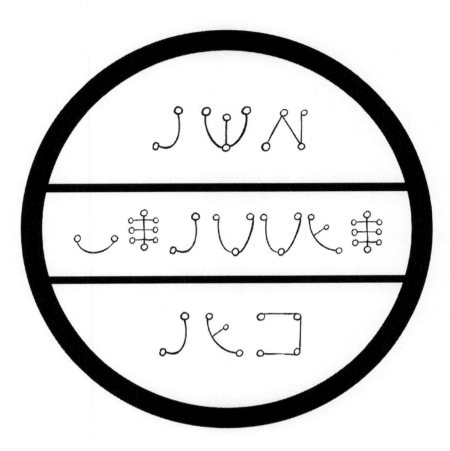

Hezi (HEZ-EE)

Ari (AH-REE)

Arneniel (ARE-NEN-EE-ELL)

EYE

10. The Angel Kawzibiah

The Quality of Hope

The Quality of Hope is an energy state that connects you to authentic possibilities, rather than pure fantasy. This means it is an energy that can help you to see your way out of a problem, rather than resorting to wishful thinking. Instead of burying your head in the sand, you will have an energy that enables you to see a true way forward, whatever the problem.

By summoning this quality, you induce an energy that can bring a sense of relief during difficult times, and clarity regarding a problem or complex situation. If your life is going quite well and there are no major problems, the energy of hope can bring more joy to your life and charisma to your personality.

Kawzibiah

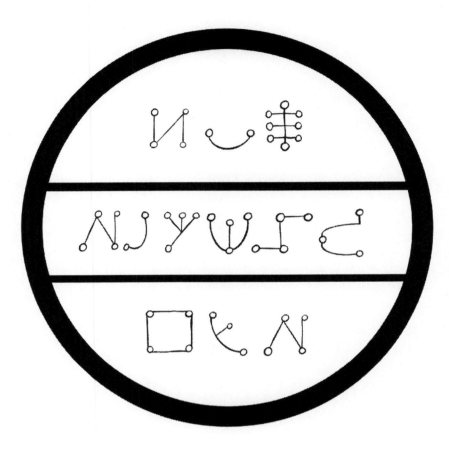

Elad (ELL-ADD)

Harach (HAH-RAHK)

Kawzibiah (CAW-ZEE-BEE-AH)

OH

11. The Angel Dahkeriah

The Quality of Integrity

The Quality of Integrity is an energy state that enables you to operate in the world in a way that accesses the truth of your talents. If you don't know your talents, you will discover them. If you know your talents, you will be able to develop them. If you wish to be better known for your abilities, integrity is an energy that attracts followers, fans, and an authentic level of support. This is not a trick for becoming famous, but a way of attracting attention and success based on tapping into the integrity of your creative or commercial work. When you believe in what you do, others will believe as well.

By summoning this quality, you induce an energy that repels enemies, detractors, and critics. There is no way to avoid all the hate that can be spread about you, especially in an era of anonymous and easy criticism, but by building the energy of integrity, your enemies and detractors will lose the will to fight or criticise you.

Dahkeriah

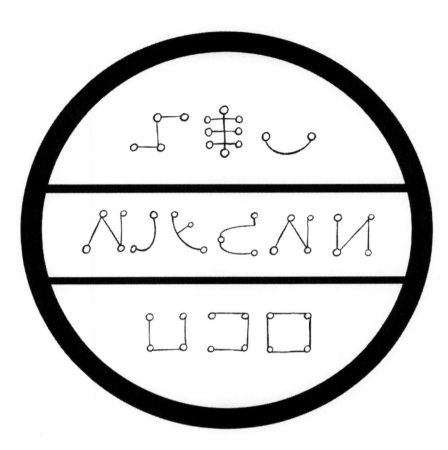

Lav (LAHV)

Chaam (KAH-AHM)

Dahkeriah (DAH-KEH-REE-AH)

EH

12. The Angel Iahemiel

The Quality of Expression

The Quality of Expression is an energy state that enables you to connect with the flow of artistic expression. It is an energy that builds on your inner passion, where you create with a sense of love for your work.

By summoning this quality, you induce an energy that will make others passionate about your creative work. A side effect is that you may appear more mysterious and alluring to other people. You will also be an inspiration to others, who sense the power of your creative expression. If you are a public speaker or need to express yourself in an interview, presentation, or other commercial situation, this energy will bring a passion and truth to your expression.

Iahemiel

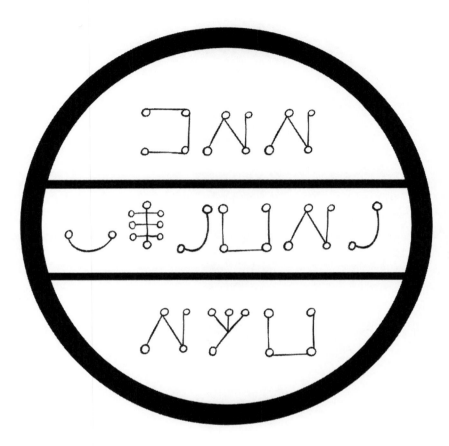

Haha (HAH-HAH)

Mivah (MEE-VAH)

Iahemiel (EE-AH-EM-EE-ELL)

EH

13. The Angel Gahbeliah

The Quality of Completion

The Quality of Completion is an energy state that enables any project you are working on to reach a state of completion more rapidly. If you are working on something – whether it is an artwork, a business plan, or some other project that matters to you – your energetic connection to the project will expand. This doesn't mean you become overwhelmed, but that your energy becomes more focussed and you are able to take the project to its conclusion with more clarity than would otherwise be possible.

By summoning this quality, you induce an energy that brings an inner strength that improves endurance and reduces the likelihood of burnout. It enables you to flourish and find focus despite interruptions, and will make those who discourage you less distracting.

Gahbeliah

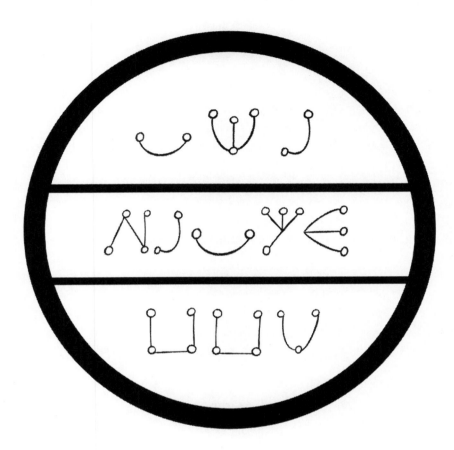

Yezel (YEH-ZELL)

Nemem (NEM-EM)

Gahbeliah (GAH-BELL-EE-AH)

AH

14. The Angel Rahdahdiel

The Quality of Belonging

The Quality of Belonging is an energy state that enables you to attract authentic friendship. Although this may seem like an unattractive power, there are few in this book that could be as important in our current social climate. It's been established that we need several close friends and a wide social circle, but most people are isolated by circumstance, addiction to devices, and an unwillingness to connect. The energy of belonging will make you a beacon of friendship so that other people want to make eye contact with you, listen to you and be listened to, and form a level of trust that is required for true friendship. Raising this energy state won't make people knock on your door and ask to be friends, but it will improve the quality of friendships (or make you see they lack true depth) while encouraging new connections with people when you put yourself in social situations.

By summoning this quality, you induce an energy that conquers loneliness and meaninglessness, by making you feel connected to your own appeal, your own goodness, and your right to be welcomed by others. This power is explained here as a way of attracting friendship, but it can also be used when you wish to be welcomed into a group, or accepted by people who are otherwise closed off to newcomers. With careful thought, this power has many practical applications.

Rahdahdiel

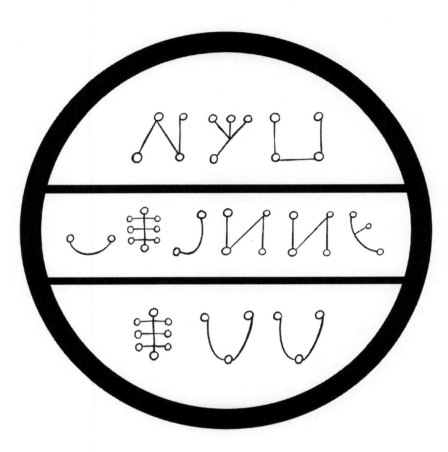

Mebah (MEB-AH)

Nena (NEN-AH)

Rahdahdiel (RAH-DAH-DEE-ELL)

EYE

15. The Angel Kemashiel

The Quality of Intuition

The Quality of Intuition is an energy state that increases your ability to be intuitive. The energy state does require input from you, so you cannot just perform the ritual and expect to be more intuitive. Although that may happen, you should move your focus to omens, synchronicities, and try to sense your feelings before you look to your rational thoughts. If you make this effort, the energy state will respond in an extremely powerful way. Trust this energy and you will become strongly intuitive.

By summoning this quality, you induce an energy that makes others more likely to trust your decisions, commands (should you be in the position to give orders), and your judgement. It will also increase your ability to trust your decision-making process, and will balance intuition with rational thought. You may also find that you obtain many flashes of insight, memories that appear from nowhere, and ideas that appear random; if you take note of these and welcome them, you may see patterns emerging. This is your inner self communicating to you through intuition, and the messages you receive can be all the guidance you need to improve your life.

Kemashiel

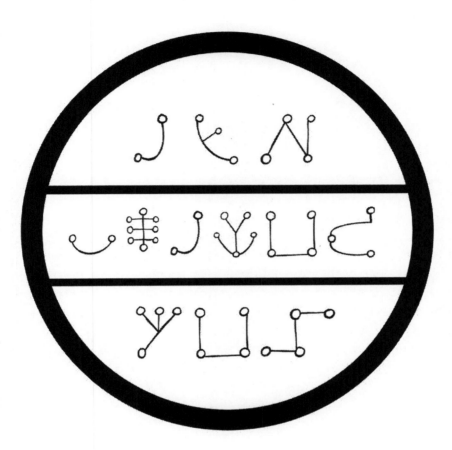

Hari (HAH-REE)

Umab (OO-MAHB)

Kemashiel (KEM-AH-SHE-ELL)

OH

16. The Angel Hahdarmiel

The Quality of Perception

The Quality of Perception is an energy state that increases your awareness of the ordinary senses, as well as your ability to perceive the future. This can be seen as an ongoing intuition or can be used to enhance deliberate attempts to see the future, through rituals or divination.

By summoning this quality, you induce an energy that also has a healing power, in that it enables you to see the truth of a hurtful situation. In this energy state, contemplate a situation that has brought you harm, and you will receive such perspective that you feel relief and healing. The energy state will improve your ability to appreciate beauty, which is considered by many to be an important aspect of being empowered. It will also support your ability to see more detail and detect patterns which can be useful in many areas of research, study, and investigation.

Hahdarmiel

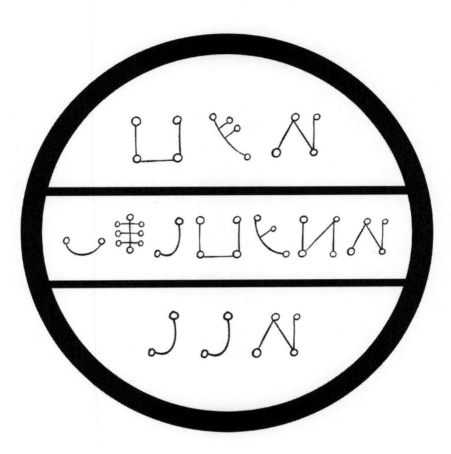

Hakem (HAK-EM)

Hayi (HAH-YEE)

Hahdarmiel (HAH-DAR-ME-ELL)

EH

17. The Angel Rabeniel

The Quality of Communication

The Quality of Communication is an energy state that enables communication which is educational or artistic. If you wish to teach what you have learned, or write a book on a subject you understand well, this energy state will enhance your ability to communicate your ideas. When expressing an idea through art, whether that is based on emotion, meaning, or reason, the idea will be clearer when empowered by this energy.

By summoning this quality, you induce an energy that draws wise people into your life, makes you more likely to perceive your own true needs, and improves your ability to be inventive and innovative in all matters.

Rabeniel

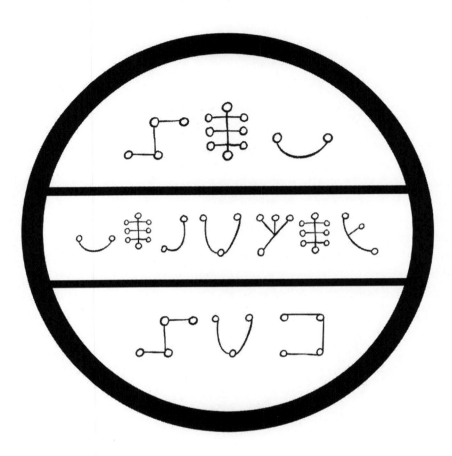

Lav (LAH-VAH)

Anu (AH-NOO)

Rabeniel (RAB-EN-EE-ELL)

OO

18. The Angel Pedahiel

The Quality of Grandeur

The Quality of Grandeur is an energy state that makes you feel like somebody who is worthy of respect, and in turn, makes others perceive you as somebody who should be appreciated and rewarded. This is not an energy of extreme ego, but a state where you feel a strong presence of power from within, and others will sense this strength.

By summoning this quality, you induce an energy that repels enemies and attracts admirers. It can help you to appreciate what you have, bringing such satisfaction that you are able to make grand goals that would once have seemed impossible. If you need the courage and stability to take another leap forward, this energy state will give you that courage. If you are entering competitions, or work in a competitive industry, the energy will make you much more likely to win awards or be rewarded for your efforts.

Pedahiel

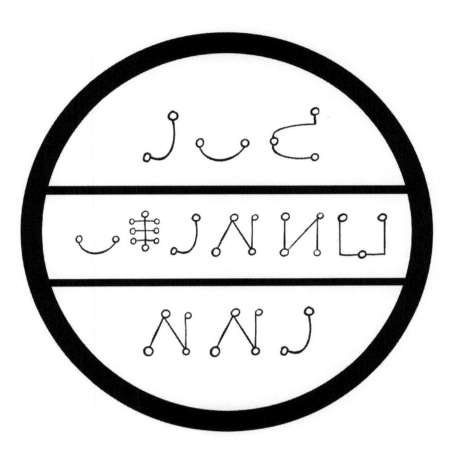

Keli (KELL-EE)

Yahah (EE-AH-AH)

Pedahiel (PED-AH-EE-ELL)

EE

19. The Angel Goramiah

The Quality of Synchronicity

The Quality of Synchronicity is an energy state that makes you able to attract and perceive significant and meaningful moments of coincidence. Where coincidence once seemed like something trivial, this energy will open you to the meaning and guidance that can be obtained through moments of synchronicity. If you work with other forms of magick and seek answers to questions, you will be more likely to find them through moments of synchronicity. If you do not use other magick, you will find that you become aware of connections, patterns, and meanings that were previously impossible for you to see. The more attention you pay to synchronicity, the more you will be rewarded for that attention, and it will begin to feel that existence itself communicates important messages to you through moments of seeming coincidence.

By summoning this quality, you induce an energy that will make you more likely to experience chance encounters that have a positive, beneficial, or meaningful effect on you. Chance meetings are more likely to carry significance. Dreams will become more meaningful. If you ever wish to make life more magickal, so that you feel connected to the universe, rather than a passenger, this energy will enable you to feel integrated with the hidden meaning where the ordinary is revealed to be far from ordinary.

Goramiah

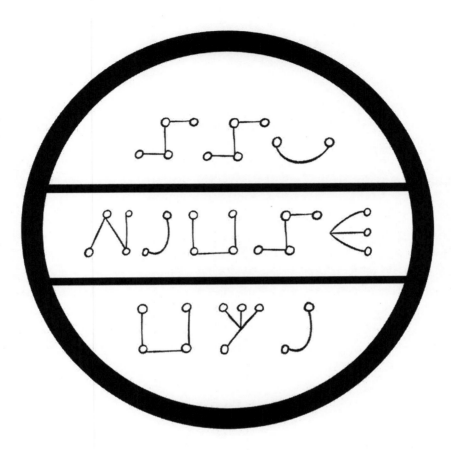

Lov (LAWV)

Yabam (YAH-BAHM)

Goramiah (GORE-AH-ME-AH)

OO

20. The Angel Ashenviel

The Quality of Esteem

The Quality of Esteem is an energy state where your resolute sense of your true self is strong enough to overcome doubts, fears, and confusion about who you are. For somebody who experiences low self-esteem, this energy will remove thought habits and deep feelings that make it difficult to feel a sense of esteem.

By summoning this quality, you induce an energy that makes it easy to feel like you are a good and worthy person, which in turn makes it easier to drop bad habits, give up unhealthy thought patterns and activities, take on new projects with courage, and overcome self-doubt.

Ashenviel

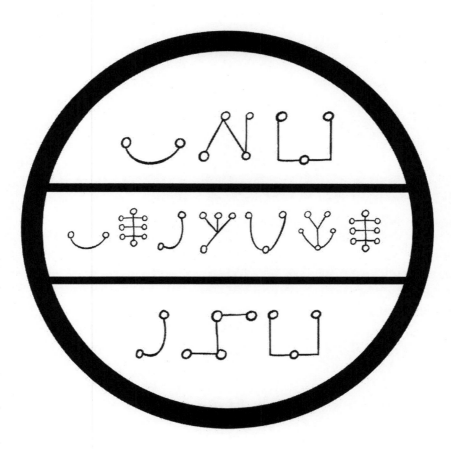

Pahal (PAH-HAHL)

Poi (PAW-EE)

Ashenviel (ASH-EN-AH-VEE-ELL)

AH

21. The Angel Periviel

The Quality of Revolution

The Quality of Revolution is an energy state that brings about rapid change. When an aspect of your life is already changing, it will increase the speed of the change. If an aspect of your life is frozen, the energy will release it, and allow change to begin. This is an energy that can be called on, not out of impatience, but out of the will to make change occur in accordance with your desire, and in alignment with your actions.

By summoning this quality, you induce an energy that makes any situation more liable to change, when you direct your attention to that area of your life. It can also reverse bad luck, bring strength where there was weakness, and urge somebody close to you to make a decision that has been resisted for too long. While the energy brings no disruption other than the change you seek, people around you may sense that you appear to be more energised, more open to change, and perhaps even more exciting. This may thrill some people but can unnerve others.

Rapid change means you will have to react and respond to changes more rapidly, so be certain that you are prepared for such change.

Periviel

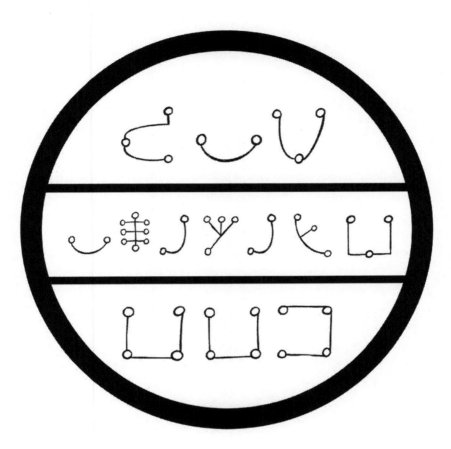

Nelach (NELL-AK)

Omem (AWE-MEM)

Periviel (PEH-REE-VEE-ELL)

OO

22. The Angel Abremviah

The Quality of Solitude

The Quality of Solitude is an energy state that makes you feel the strength within yourself, regardless of how others are. You may not be alone, but you will be at peace with yourself. This energy can be extremely calming and centering, even when you are surrounded by others.

By summoning this quality, you induce an energy that can be used to repel negative or unwanted people from your life. The cruel and critical will lose interest in you, and you will be able to achieve a sense of personal strength whatever the circumstances are in your life. If you need to be introspective, this energy will enable that. If you need to feel at one with yourself, without being lonely, you can enjoy that feeling. If you are lonely, a time spent enjoying the strength of solitude can be the best way to prepare for new friendships and relationships.

Abremviah

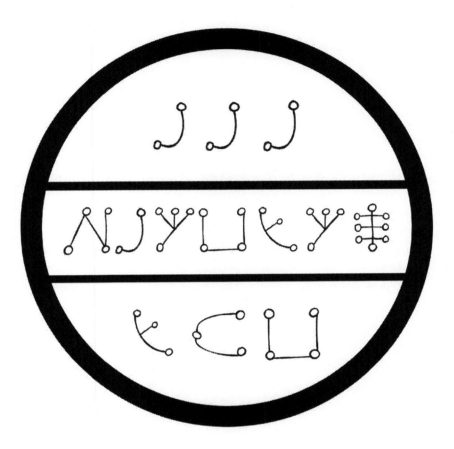

Yeyay (YEH-YAH-EE)

Metzer (MET-ZAIR)

Abremviah (AB-REM-VEE-AH)

AH

23. The Angel Adashniah

The Quality of Fascination

The Quality of Fascination is an energy state that brings a joyous clarity to your thoughts and perceptions. Instead of being dulled by heavy, slow energies of doubt and cynicism, you reconnect with your innate ability to see the beauty, truth, and potential of people, places, and situations.

By summoning this quality, you induce an energy that gives you clear thought, without apprehension, so that you can think, work, communicate, or create in ways that are inspired and refreshing. The energy state can make people more likely to admire you for all that you do, say, and achieve. If you are creative, others will be fascinated by your work, and by you.

Adashniah

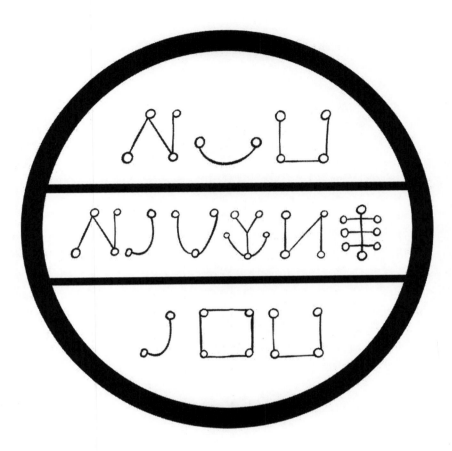

Melah (MEL-AH)

Machi (MAH-KEY)

Adashniah (ADD-AH-SHEN-EE-AH)

EE

24. The Angel Hodahdiah

The Quality of Manifestation

The Quality of Manifestation is an energy state in which anything you seek to attract is more likely to come into your life. This does not mean you can induce the energy state and expect all your wishes to come true. But when you have been working towards a goal, this energy state can cause it to break through into manifestation.

By summoning this quality, you induce an energy that makes new realities more likely. It makes all of reality more subject to change, and when you impose your will on reality, whether through direct effort or through magick, your efforts will be more effective. The key to using this magick is good timing. Used too early, when something is not quite ready to manifest, it may be too soon to have a strong effect. Use it too late, and you might have missed the opportunity to sway reality. Although it is potentially one of the most powerful energies in the book, it takes more skill than the others, so be prepared to practice and learn.

Hodahdiah

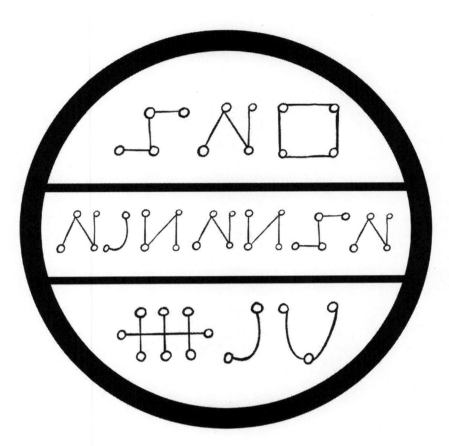

Chaho (KAH-HAW)

Nit (NEAT)

Hodahdiah (HAW-DAH-DEE-AH)

EYE

25. The Angel Televemiel

The Quality of Justice

The Quality of Justice is an energy state that makes you impervious to the attempts of others to damage your name or reputation. This quality will make slanderous statements, gossip, and rumours go unheard or unheeded, so that you will maintain your reputation. If you are in a difficult legal situation, the energy will also ensure that you will be seen for who and what you are. Attempts to make you look worse than you are will fail.

By summoning this quality, you induce an energy that makes others see who you are without prejudice, so that they form opinions about you based on facts or authentic intuition, rather than on falsehoods. This energy state helps ensure that you attract justice when others speak ill of you, or when dealing with legal problems.

Televemiel

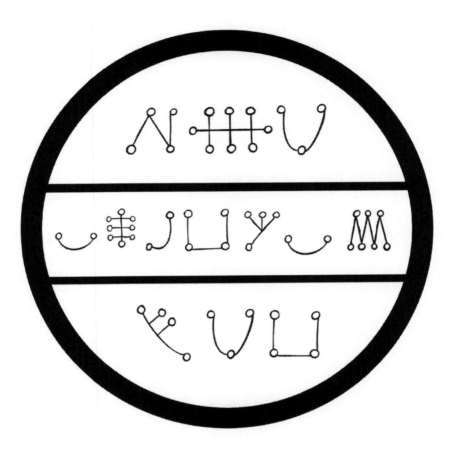

Netah (NET-AH)

Menak (MEN-AHK)

Televemiel (TEH-LEV-EM-EE-ELL)

OO

26. The Angel Ikapetiah

The Quality of Discovery

The Quality of Discovery is an energy state that helps you see the best course of action to take, both in the immediate future and for long-term benefits. This quality, when used at times of great change, or when seeking to make a shift in your life, can bring you the ability to discover a new pathway through life that will get you where you want to be.

By summoning this quality, you induce an energy that makes it easier to understand what you want, and helps to remove confusion. If there is an area of life that you find confusing, the energy can be directed there to help you discover a new way of seeing that situation.

Ikapetiah

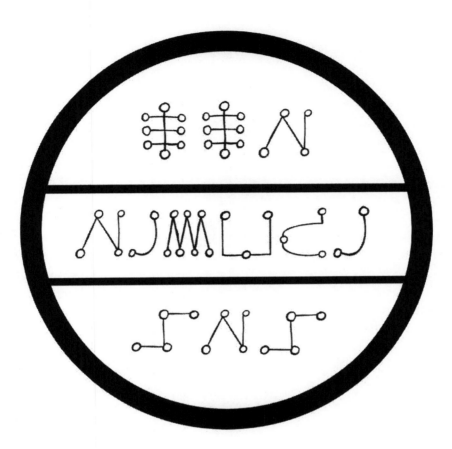

Haah (HAH-AH)

Vehu (VEH-WHO)

Ikapetiah (EE-KAH-PET-EE-AH)

OH

27. The Angel Marenshiel

The Quality of Resolve

The Quality of Resolve is an energy state that increases your connection to whatever it is you wish to achieve. With this energy, any commitment you make is more like a vow, and you will be more likely to see it through to completion. If you plan to undertake a major project, this energy can be an excellent way to help make the commitment feel real to you.

By summoning this quality, you induce an energy that makes you highly aware of vows and commitments, so that you can see which are still wanted, and which you wish to be released from your life. If you wish to release them, the energy will make that easier to achieve.

You may also find that when you are filled with this energy, those who know you or encounter you will be awed by your presence because they can sense your resolve. You will appear to be somebody with vision, or a great leader. Sometimes, you may wish to use the energy state precisely to convey this impression.

Marenshiel

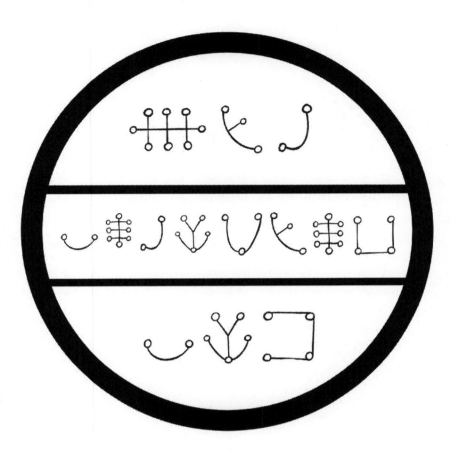

Yeret (YEH-RET)

Eshal (ESH-AHL)

Marenshiel (MAR-EN-SHE-ELL)

AH

28. The Angel Napemiah

The Quality of Renewal

The Quality of Renewal is an energy state in which you are cleansed of the thoughts and feelings that keep you from being at one with your passions, your calling, or your highest skills and abilities.

By summoning this quality, you induce an energy that can ease anxious or clouded thought. The energy can make everything that prevents you from moving forward, fall away. In this state of renewal, you will discover old passions and new passions, as well as being clearer about what you want from life. If you only have a general sense of being held back by unwanted habits and thoughts, the energy will work. If there is an area of your life that feels particularly blocked, you can focus the energy there, to ensure that you seek renewal in that part of your life.

Napemiah

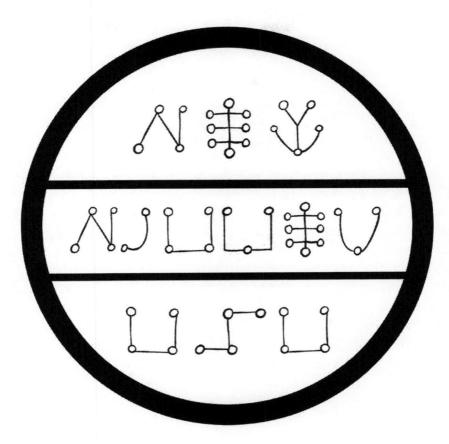

Shahah (SHAH-AH)

Mum (MOOM)

Napemiah (NAP-EM-EE-AH)

EH

29. The Angel Aremotiel

The Quality of Peace

The Quality of Peace is an energy state where you experience peace even when the world around you is not at peace. When your emotions or your circumstances are far from peaceful, the energy will enable you to experience peace. This can bring renewal, and ability to persevere, or just the pleasant joy of being at peace with yourself despite the state of your world. When you experience this peace, the state of your world may seem less disastrous, and problems often rectify themselves. It is one of the most powerful energies in this book.

By summoning this quality, you induce an energy that can bring an end to conflict or argument, attracting kindness from others. Pain can be replaced by pleasure, and evil thoughts that are held against you will dissolve when confronted by the light of peace within you.

Aremotiel

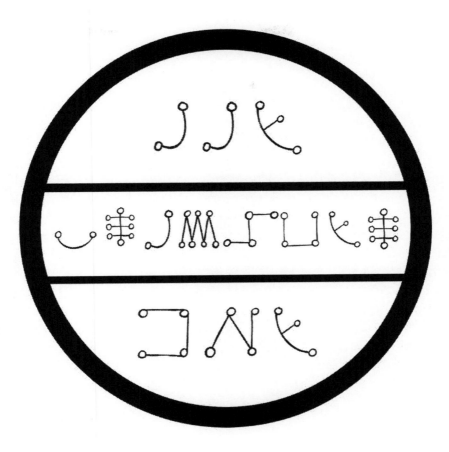

Riyi (REE-YEE)

Reho (REH-HAW)

Aremotiel (ARE-EM-AWE-TEE-ELL)

EE

30. The Angel Radekiel

The Quality of Honesty

The Quality of Honesty is an energy state that can help you be honest with yourself, or can encourage and compel others to be honest with you. This is a quality that could be underestimated, but it has more potential than you may realise until used. You will never become more honest than you want to be, blurting out secrets, but if you want to be honest in your self-perception, or in your expression to another person, this energy will make that easy for you. If you want somebody else to be more honest, when you doubt their sincerity, the energy will encourage that openness from other people.

By summoning this quality, you induce an energy that can increase your sense of belonging, whether with friends, family, at work, or in other social and collective situations. Strangely, the energy can also help you keep a secret you have been entrusted with. If you seek to know the truth of an important matter, the energy will help improve your perception of truth.

Radekiel

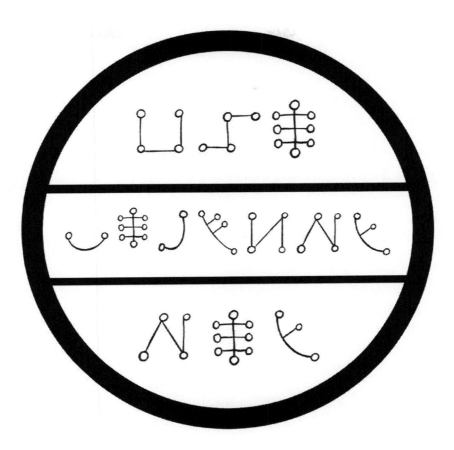

Oma (AWE-MAH)

Raah (RAH-AH)

Radekiel (RAH-DECK-EE-ELL)

OO

31. The Angel Temarkiel

The Quality of Forgiveness

The Quality of Forgiveness is an energy state which gives you immense strength and a return to joy when you have been wronged. Without the need to harm others, prove a point, or set the record straight, you will be able to forgive those who have harmed you, recently or from long ago. This deliberate act of forgiveness, while in the energy state, can produce an immense feeling of freedom and opens up energy blockages that may have prevented your life and your magick from progressing.

By summoning this quality, you induce an energy that will end wicked thoughts that others may hold, so that they forgive you (regardless of whether their anger was justified or not.) The energy can also reduce spite in a relationship while bringing trust, mercy, and understanding from all the people you meet and interact with. It can help you to be present during a conversation, making you a good listener, but can also make those you converse with more willing to listen when you want to be heard.

Temarkiel

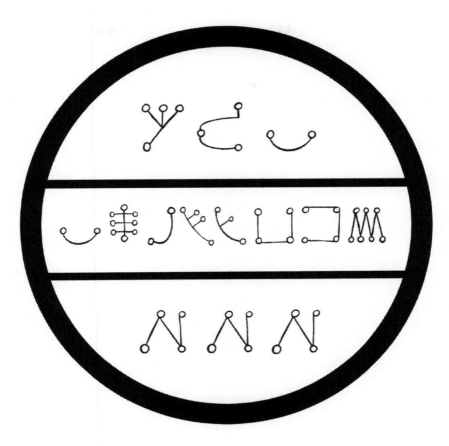

Lecav (LEK-AHV)

Hahah (HAH-HAH-AH)

Temarkiel (TEM-ARE-KEY-ELL)

EH

32. The Angel Aledekiel

The Quality of Contemplation

The Quality of Contemplation is an energy state that puts you into a state of elegant communication with your inner self. This power can be used when you want to think or contemplate so that you are able to make authentic decisions. It can make you impervious to distractions or people who would otherwise drain you of energy.

By summoning this quality, you induce an energy that can improve your memory, which can be useful in ordinary life, or for a special occasion, such as learning for an exam. The energy makes you able to speak more clearly, reducing nervous energy and giving you the ability to communicate well when speaking. If your health has suffered, and you have begun to recover, the energy of contemplation can be restorative, speeding up your recovery time.

Aledekiel

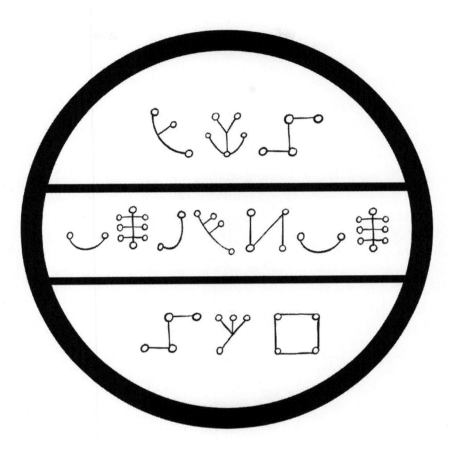

Vesher (VESH-AIR)

Chavu (KAH-VOO)

Aledekiel (AL-ED-ECK-EE-EL)

EYE

33. The Angel Kenoriah

The Quality of Stillness

The Quality of Stillness is an energy state that brings incredible focus and presence in the moment. Stillness is not a lack of energy, but a connection to the vitality of the present moment.

By summoning this quality, you induce an energy that can ease your reactions to people and situations. If you are compulsive, this energy can help you break that habit. This energy of stillness can also help you convey power in a way that makes others less willing to bully, oppress, or otherwise bother you. If you seek silence, quiet, and freedom from distraction, this energy will attract those conditions, or make you able to achieve focus even when surrounded by clamour.

Kenoriah

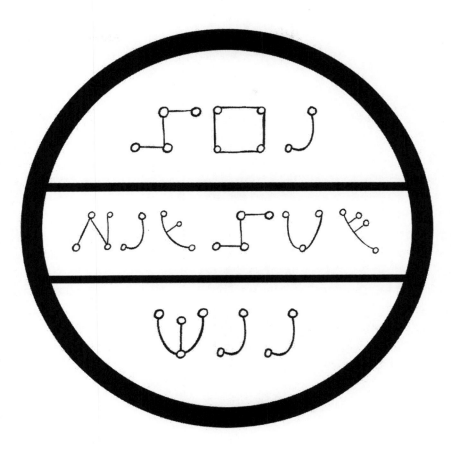

Yichu (YEE-KOO)

Yeyiz (YEH-EASE)

Kenoriah (KEN-AWE-REE-AH)

AH

34. The Angel Arkapiah

The Quality of Allowing

The Quality of Allowing is an energy state that enables you to accept the things you want, without impatience, urgency, or desperation. When you seek to change your life, too much desperate need can make it impossible to enjoy the gifts magick can offer. In a state of allowing, you are much more likely to manifest anything you seek.

By summoning this quality, you induce an energy that will help to prevent over-thinking, resistance to change, or attachment to old ways. If you find that you are impatient for change, or 'lusting for results,' that impatience can take away the power of magick. Get into a state of allowing, through this energy state, and you will free yourself of this urgent lust. When you become free of urgency, results of all kinds will come to you more readily.

Arkapiah

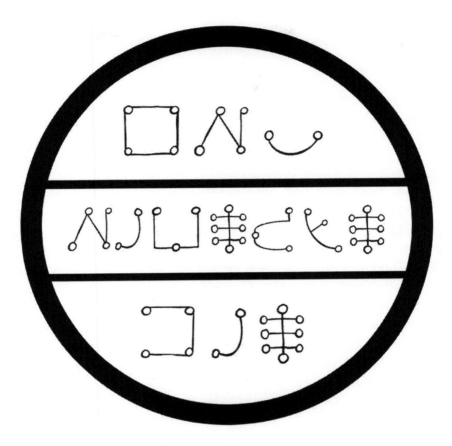

Lehach (LEH-HACK)

Iya (EE-YAH)

Arkapiah (ARK-AH-PEE-AH)

OH

35. The Angel Marmahshiel

The Quality of Inspiration

The Quality of Inspiration is an energy state that makes it possible to become more receptive to ideas and new ways of thinking. It can be used when you are seeking answers, working creatively, or when looking for inspiration for a new direction to take in your life.

By summoning this quality, you induce an energy that will remove cynicism, doubt, and the heavy thoughts of fear. In a state of inspiration, you may find that you experience greater love, as you are inspired to notice connections between yourself and others. When seeking ideas, or working on any project, the chances of being inspired in a creative and effective way are greatly increased. If you are working on something that has lost its lustre, this energy can renew your interest by revealing what there could still be for you to discover. For anybody experiencing writer's block, or a similar artistic struggle, there could be many other causes and other types of magick that apply, but a boost of inspiration will usually be helpful and can break you out of a frozen state.

Some people find that inspiration also brings courage to create or begin new projects, as the energy is not just one of ideas, but comes with the sense that these ideas have the power to manifest. When you are inspired by this energy, you know that whatever you wish to create can become real.

Marmahshiel

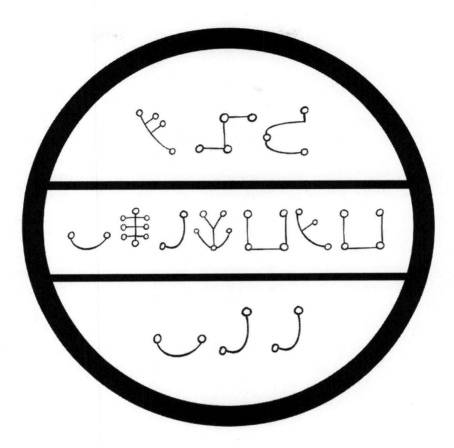

Kevek (KEV-ECK)

Yeyil (YEH-YEEL)

Marmahshiel (MAR-MAH-SHE-ELL)

EE

36. The Angel Sekeshiah

The Quality of Abundance

The Quality of Abundance is an energy state that brings ease to attainment. Abundance is a state where you attain what you need without struggle. This does not mean that riches fall into your hands as soon as you perform a ritual, but that when you actively seek prosperity, or when you need to manifest money, the energy of abundance makes it easier to obtain what you desire. In a state of abundance, you are free of the fear of going without, and this makes it easier to obtain more.

By summoning this quality, you induce an energy that gives courage when you begin or progress with a venture. It removes your fear about losing what you have and makes it easier to feel that you will obtain all you need. This enables a more trusting feeling of tranquil acceptance, enabling your enjoyment of the present to make way for you to receive more, in material terms.

Sekeshiah

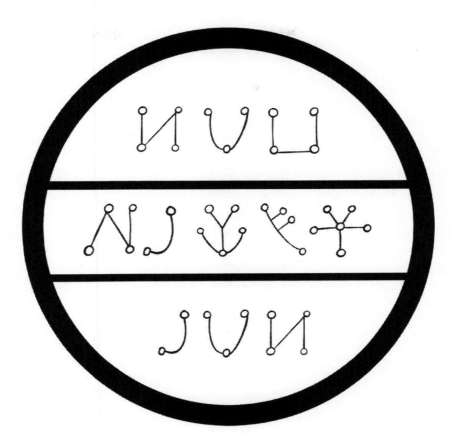

Menad (MEN-AHD)

Dani (DAH-NEE)

Sekeshiah (SEK-ESH-EE-AH)

OO

The Discovery of Magick

Where do these angels come from? In reviews of occult books, in questions on websites, and in forums, people ask; *What is magick? How does it work? Where do the angels come from?* The questions may be brought about by casual curiosity, serious interest, or fear.

Every book of practical magick is born of a thousand other books, with hundreds of personal contributions from fellow occultists over many decades, thousands of years of history and experimentation, and practical experience. Nothing matters as much as experience, and personal discussions have been vital to me, but I would be nowhere without the books I have read.

Often, people request a bibliography, almost as though they want proof, and as though a list of books could provide that proof. It cannot, and as I have said before, such a list will only be the merest glimpse of what I have read and experienced. I sometimes feel it would be easier to say, 'I've read almost everything about magick,' because that is closer to the truth than a limited bibliography. It is reasonable, however, for a reader to wonder where this all comes from.

A complete bibliography would be impossible for me to compile due to its extreme length. I would surely forget many important texts, and could not possibly list every book that has influenced my journey to this book. Many books I have encountered are difficult to read unless you have the assistance of a translator and access to a good library, with many hours to spare, and in this regard, I am grateful for the assistance I received from those who mentored me. I am also grateful for the privately held grimoires which inform these works. It grows tiresome to hear occult authors talk of 'private collections,' but if you do much research, you will find that even the major academic writers don't get far without consulting books held in private collections. These personal grimoires are often just notebooks, and at other times, they are important texts that are central to our understanding of magick. No bibliography can make meaningful sense of those texts, and although it may sound fanciful to speak of them, they have their place, as will be elucidated in what remains of this chapter.

When looking into the history of angels you will see there are only a small number of angels named in the Bible, and readers who are new to magick become concerned when they find that angel names are usually derived from Kabbalistic documents, which were in turn influenced by ancient texts, and sources such as *The Book of Enoch*. These sources are unfamiliar, and that can make them feel strange.

Other readers have little concern about such origins, perform the magick, and get what they want. If you do the magick as written in my books, it works, unless you ask for the outrageous, but it is perhaps worth considering the recent developments in modern occultism, to show that some knowledge of origins can be valuable. You don't need an entire history of magick to get what you want, but sometimes, you want more than the author's reassurance that everything is valid.

To illustrate how confusion and doubt can cause problems, I will look back to the time when I was still deeply involved in magickal research. It was a time when academic work plodded on slowly, but occultists (for a short time) shared their secrets in popular books, much as is happening in recent years. It was the seventies, and the birth of semi-popular occultism. Former secrets were shared in pamphlets and books. Some were wonderful, but others were less than spectacular. One that remains popular today, largely because it has been pirated so widely, is *The Miracle of New Avatar Power* by Geof Gray-Cobb. The book contained (amongst other things) a ritual-closing method where you traced shapes with your fingers while saying the word DEE-HAY-THOOTH. The origin and meaning of this phrase were not explained in his book, so it was debated for many decades, especially when online forums became popular, and the general consensus was that this was a Thelema-style call to the Egyptian god Thoth. This is absolutely incorrect.

When Gray-Cobb's book was first available, I guarantee most readers had no idea what the phrase DEE-HAY-THOOTH meant. Even today, you hear some wild explanations for its origins. The phrase has a quite ordinary origin, being created by a female author, not that long ago. During my ongoing research into magick, I found that the phrase and the ritual from *The Miracle of New Avatar Power* appears to be based on workings from a book called *The Armour of Light* by Olive Pixley, originating from 1957. It's not ancient, Egyptian, or in any way exotic. It's from 1957.

Pixley spelled it as DEAY-THU-TH. Close, but not identical. The phrase was 'given' to Pixley, as she puts it, with the implication from her writings being that it was obtained through a vision, trance, or a form of channelling, and it has no origin other than her personal experience. There is no dusty old book from centuries ago that we can point to and say it's real because it was written down a long time ago. It was written down in 1957.

Pixley came to believe that DEAY-THU-TH was an Aramaic form of the name Jesus, although the evidence for this was sketchy at best. What is notable, however, is that Pixley's magic word was channelled only to her and has no other source. It did not originate from an ancient document, or through word of mouth or from private occult documents. It came to her in a vision. This does not make it invalid, but that fact may come as a surprise to readers of *The Miracle of New Avatar Power*. They think they are using an ancient magickal word from Egypt!

Pixley's ritual method that went with the word included a process whereby the syllables were spoken while visualizing a blue triangle being drawn behind the head, a blue chalice appearing above the head (filled with light), and a line of light descending through the body, culminating in a spiral that felt like a small pulse in the abdomen. The syllables were to be spoken with specific in-breaths and out-breaths, at varying volumes. These were quite specific instructions.

There is no doubt in my mind that the ritual in *The Miracle of New Avatar Power* was based on Pixley's material, because it contains the same components: triangle, chalice shape with the line ending in a spiral, and a word that sounds very similar, but Gray-Cobb's description is much more basic and stripped bare. It contains a tracing of the shapes with an extended arm, a change in pronunciation, and an absence of other details. It looks like a rehash of what Pixley created.

For decades many lone occultists were using the slightly incorrect pronunciation of DEE-HAY-THOOTH (instead of DEAY-THU-TH), assuming they were calling on Thoth when they were actually saying a word that the ritual-creator believed to be Jesus, even though it might not mean Jesus at all. This is quite a muddle.

What are we to make of this garbled history? My observation is that the DEE-HAY-THOOTH ritual from Gray-Cobb's book has not been very effective for most occultists, and this may be because his version is so far removed from the Pixley 'original'. As to whether her original method works, even that is quite debatable, as it was not widely practiced, and because it originates from one person, it may not translate well to being used by others.

A process that modern occultists take part in is the reprocessing and simplification of old rituals into forms that are still workable. While some may say Gray-Cobb was plagiarizing, I think it is fair to say that in this case, he was trying to create something new based on what he had read and experienced. But I believe he had reworked Pixley's material too far, and by providing absolutely no background material to readers, or showing where the word came from or what it meant, those readers were left in the dark as to the intent behind the ritual.

If he had said, 'You are closing your ritual by saying *Jesus* and empowering His name with these shapes,' the readers would have at least known what they were dealing with. Most who use it, even today, have no idea they are using 'Jesus magick.'

It would also help if the readers knew this magick did not originate, as many assumed, from ancient Egyptian texts, but from a woman in England who came up with the idea just a few decades ago.

I believe Gray-Cobb's *New Avatar Power* book was an attempt at basic, practical magick, which I support, but the book was filled with strange mispronunciations (most of the angels' names were outrageously incorrect), over-simplification and calls to some entities that were reckless and, in my opinion, potentially harmful. The magick worked some of the time for some people, so it remains popular despite its flaws. In the case of the DEE-HAY-THOOTH ritual, he may only have wasted readers' time by providing something that did nothing. I do find it troubling, however, that he referred to this as an evocation, because the idea of evoking Jesus to appear before you is more than reckless. Perhaps he was using language loosely, or perhaps he never knew about the Jesus connection.

In exploring this, I am not insisting that Pixley's work was without value, or that its hasty reconstruction in the seventies by Gray-Cobb was completely worthless. That is for the users of the material to decide. The point of this small history is to show that when no sources are given, and no background information provided, it is easy for the operator of the magick to get confused ideas about the *intention* of the work. Calling out to Thoth is very different from saying the name of Jesus.

Perhaps this doesn't matter at all if it works, but I know that many readers were drawn to the Egyptian overtones they sensed in *New Avatar Power*, without knowing they were using a modern form of Christian magick, along with some extremely distorted Greek and Hebrew. In truth, none of this would matter if it wasn't for online piracy and a shortage of useful, practical texts. When so little was available, readers took what they could get, whether it was legal or not. Now, many authors have released work that has the benefit of fifty more years of magickal research behind it, but it remains the case that sources are rarely explored in detail.

Without *some* understanding, some people find it can be difficult to work with magick effectively. You do not need to know the entire history of magick, but it helps if you know what the ritual is actually *for*. This is the most important thing to know; it's more important than origins or meanings of words, but sometimes writers present their material in a way that means you don't know what it's even for. After reading *The Miracle of New Avatar Power*, I had no concept of what the DEE-HAY-THOOTH ritual was meant to do other than a vague promise that it could add some 'power' to a ritual. That was too abstract.

This is why I endeavour to show how magick can be used. Knowing what it's *for* is as important as its origin.

Origins are important, even if only to the author. This story of Pixley and Gray-Cobb is meant to illustrate the difficulties that modern occultists have when it comes to supplying material to readers. We need to find a balance between knowledge and heavy-handedness, but should at least let readers know what the magick is for, and how it can be used.

To provide another example, the 'secret magick word,' MA-RA appeared in several texts during the last half-century, most famously in a book published in 1985. It was said this lost word was known only to adepts and had been kept from the public, and could help you achieve many miraculous results. Perhaps it can. What exactly these results were meant to be was not made clear enough for me. Was it a good luck charm, or a way of calling on spirits, or something else?

I have seen countless references to this word, and many claims over the decades that it was being published for the first time ever, even though it has been widely circulated well beyond living memory. Al Manning's book, *Moon Lore and Moon Magic* from 1980, covers the word MA-RA, and it appears in many other places, but there are too many to list here. With minimal research, you will find there are many references to this word from long before 1985.

Several people have shown me the 'original source,' and in each case, the 'original source was always different, showing that many who claimed to have obtained the word first were not being truthful or didn't have all the facts.

Given the number of times this so-called 'secret word' appeared as an occult revelation, both privately through personal correspondence or in publications, over many years, it is possible that it is genuinely powerful. It is also possible that it was passed on so enthusiastically only because it was *supposedly* secret, not because of what it can actually do. Without knowing the origin of the word, it is impossible to know what it's *for*.

You can, of course, take the risk and try chanting it, but without knowing its origin and purpose, who would want to do that? And this is one of those examples where I would say that without knowing the source, we have entered the realm of guesswork and experimentation. I would not be inclined to chant MA-RA until I knew what it meant and where it came from.

Although I believe a knowledge of origins is important, I am also aware that the opposite can be entirely true, which is an interesting and challenging paradox. You can *use* magick without knowing its source or meaning, and it will work. Sometimes people chant sounds that appear to be magick words, but they are actually the *names* of angels, and the results come about because the ritual process is well-structured enough for it to work. No additional knowledge is required. I still believe, however, that knowing the magickal *intent* of a ritual is important.

You may know there is a word used throughout magick that some, such as Éliphas Lévi, have even proclaimed to be the most powerful word within all magick. The word is AGLA, often pronounced AGG-LAH or AH-GAH-LAH. When used in certain states of mind, or at specific times within a ritual, this word can have tremendous power, even if you have absolutely

117

no idea what it means. It is an acronym for the words, Atah Gibor Le-olam Adonai, which are Hebrew words meaning, 'You, O Lord, are mighty forever.' Despite the simplicity of the meaning, the word AGLA is powerful, and this may be because it was constructed into an acronym for the *purpose* of magick. That is, some words are magickal because they were designed to invoke or attract magick. They are known as Words of Power.

Readers sometimes want to know what magick words mean and hope for a translation, but these magick words are often angelic names, Divine Names, or acronyms of other names and phrases, as with AGLA. Some can be translated, but most cannot be translated because they are names or constructions that go beyond language and access other levels of power. It's like asking for a translation of the number seventeen.

When writing my books, I do not explain the origin of every name and word, and this can create doubt. You may believe the names and words could have originated anywhere, and could mean anything. I am also aware that magick often works without full knowledge of the origins. It is fair to say that the background material for my books, if piled up, would be far taller than me, several times over. I am sure you don't want to work your way through that. You want to *use* magick.

Each time you work with magick to fulfil a sincere need, you sense the true origins of magick. When results come, the gratitude you feel opens you up to new ways of seeing the world. Although it has taken many paragraphs to get here, this is the point I have been building up to. If you can find the will to perform magick, you will sense everything you need to know as your life with magick begins to grow, and the results you seek manifest in your reality.

And you may still wonder where all this magick comes from. Has it been around for millennia, centuries, or just a few years? Is it unchanged or constantly modified?

Magick is constantly being invented, discovered, shaped, shared, and honed, but there is also a tradition of magick being distributed in secret. What you see happening today is that secrets from many of those previously hidden sources are being shared with the public for the first time.

In *The Keys to The Gateway of Magick*, the academic writers, Stephen Skinner and David Rankine, repeat and summarise their belief that magick does not have much to do with secret societies. They also suggest that magick was not passed down through the traditional village 'cunning-man.' Instead, they say, it was handed down from one scholar-magician to the next. This is far from my experience, and far from the experience of all those I know who work with magick.

It is no surprise that these two academic writers would believe that academics are behind all this. We can't be too surprised that they've summed up the whole history of Western magickal transmission as a practice of scholarly wisdom. They go on to add that magick tended to belong to one social class – the upper-class Establishment.

I like a lot of what they say in their book, but I think these points are laden with too much emphasis on academic study, and not enough experience of magick in the modern world.

Magick comes from many places. If you only do your research in places like the British Library, you miss the rich reality of modern magick. I have sat for many long hours in that library, but it was only when I returned to a place where I *performed* magick that I understood magick.

It's true that the Establishment *recorded* magick most effectively, being educated and in a position to do so. They wrote books and secret documents that were indeed passed between high-society friends. But that is not the whole story. If the lower classes didn't record their magick as elegantly, that has more to do with the fact that publishing was something only attainable by the elite. But if you read *The Cunning Man's Handbook* by Jim Baker (for which Rankine himself wrote a glowing Foreword), it is apparent that ordinary folk did have access to spells, sigils, and seals that were supposedly reserved for the upper classes.

I admire the way Skinner and Rankine have tried to distance practical magick from the Illuminati and Freemasonry because it is too easy and compelling a conspiracy theory to say that all magick is being used by super-powerful people who hide it to retain power. And it's not true. I know, from personal experience that people from all walks of life have access to magick, use magick, and make great gains with the magick they use. The richest and most powerful people in the world may or may not use magick, but they certainly don't control it.

Magick may have been beautifully recorded by lawyers and judges of old, as Skinner and Rankine note, but I think it is also true that magick has long been used by village occultists, as well as by secret societies composed of more ordinary people. These were people who aimed for more. These societies were (and are) small, private groups of individuals. These people are not noticeably running the world, but they are influencing aspects of our modern reality.

Magick brings power, but that power isn't always walking the corridors of Whitehall (or Congress, or anywhere else). There have been secret societies in publishing, in music, in the theatre, in trade and transport, and even education. It's not all about governments and banks. I have encountered several such societies in my life, and have been a member of more than one.

It is amusing that we often talk about the 'chaos magick movement' as being an invention of the 1970s. That is the decade when magicians boldly simplified magick and broke the rules, finding that even with lots of changes, the magick still worked. If that's what chaos magick is, then it's been going on for centuries. Although the seventies were an exciting time for readers, with more occult books being made available to the public than ever before, the simplification and refinement of magick was nothing new. While the scholar magicians passed down their secret ideas, other secrets were passed between occultists in the ordinary world. These ideas were shared and adapted, tested, and changed. They were made to work.

But who has the best magick? Is the purest magick, passed down by scholars, the best? Would you rather have the magick of a wealthy Lord or a normal businessman who's a member of some small unknown group? Remember that the power of Lords was inherited, not earned, and I think this point is often missed. Those already in power do not need the results that magick can provide as much as those who have known the struggle. The Lords and Ladies of the land may be fascinated and curious, but they do not *need* to work with magick the same way that others do.

Ordinary people who aimed for more achieved great magickal work, and they led the revolution of magick. It was clear to such people that you can rise to a certain level through hard work and ingenuity, but it was also apparent that you could not leave your social and economic class easily. Not without magick. And that's what many people did.

Modern magick is not a blurring of the truth found in ancient documents but is a genuine search for magick that works, led by people who need the results. This is more real and exciting than reading an old 'pure' document.

Much of the magick being shared today is a blend of magick from many origins. It comes from small secret societies that tested and developed the magick through personal experiment. These societies are not yet catalogued by academics, and they have drawn on many sources, creating magick that works, and I think it has reached the point where this is undeniable.

In my books, I hope to share the hidden magick that has been used, quietly and effectively, by ordinary people who seek to live in a way that is more than ordinary. I trust that when you use magick and let it become part of your life, your life will never be the same again.

Pronouncing the Names

You may be wondering exactly how to pronounce the Names, and why they are pronounced in the way that they are. When you see a Name such as Lav, you might think it should sound like the LAV in LAVATORY. So why is it sounded out as LAH-VAH?

In most books of magick, even from centuries ago, the Hebrew was written without the vowel markings. You see the main letters and are left to guess what the vowels might be. Sometimes you find vowel markings, but they are from a more recent document, meaning they could have been added for convenience. You may find the markings in older documents, and when they match up across many sources, you can be fairly certain you've found an effective pronunciation. In all cases, occultists generally find that testing out a pronunciation is what matters. When it works, it is retained, and so in this book, you get the result of such testing.

For a Name such as LAV, the practical work of occultists has shown that one of the effective pronunciations is LAH-VAH. You may notice there are actually two versions of this name, and the other is pronounced as LAHV, even though it contains the same three letters.

In some cases, it can be quite puzzling, even when you have some knowledge of the language being used. When you see a Divine Name such as Poi, you expect it to sound like the first part of POISON, but it is pronounced as PAW-EE. To understand this, you could look at the Hebrew letters, and you will find that they are Peh, Vav, and Yud. They look like this (reading from right to left, as is always the case with Hebrew):

Of course, in this book, the Hebrew letters are replaced with the Celestial Alphabet, and so they look like this:

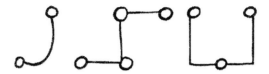

Peh, Vav, and Yud equate with the English letters P, V and I, or PVI. This might make you think it should be pronounced as PEV-EYE. How then, do we arrive at PAW-EE?

To explain, the direct letter equivalent of Vav is V, but Vav is often sounded as AWE. When written in English, Vav is written as O. This means that in Poi, the O sounds like AWE.

To illustrate this further, the letter Yud is often written as I, but it can sound like EE. When you see OI, that means you get AWE and EE. The Name Poi, therefore, sounds like PAW-EE.

If I simply wrote the Divine Name Poi, you would not know how to pronounce it, because the long traditions of converting Hebrew to English are far from obvious.

In a name such as Goramiah (GORE-AH-ME-AH) there is no letter R in the original name, but the R is suggested when the name is spoken. As such, when written in English, and with the phonetics, it is shown to have an R.

This is all quite counter-intuitive, but that's why the phonetic pronunciation guide is included. If you're confused, you don't need to be. It is this simple: say the words in block capitals, just as they are written, and it will work. Everything reads as though it's in English, but note that the G sound is always like the G in grow or give, *not* the sound you get from germ or gender.

Your pronunciation does not have to be perfect, because there is no single way to pronounce these words and Names, just as there is no single way to pronounce your name.

Everybody says these Names differently, and the visual content of the sigil overrides any mistakes you might make.

It is also apparent that *attempting* to make the right sound appears to create the required effect. Whatever the nature of your voice, the quality of your accent, or the strength of your speech, sounding out the Names as shown will work.

This section was included only to clarify a few points that might worry readers who think something is wrong, missing, or confusing. Use the magick without concern or fear that you are making a mistake, and that feeling of certainty brings far more power than any attempt to perfect your pronunciation.

How Magick is Shared

by Chris Wood

Thank you for buying this book. I am proud to release another book by Ben Woodcroft. I consider him to be one of the best occult writers of modern times.

The Power of Magick Publishing has now published a few modern classics, and I hope to keep publishing occult books in the coming years. I appreciate your support, as do the authors.

As a reader, I hope you feel you get good value from these books. If you enjoyed *The Angel Overlords*, please write a review on Amazon or Goodreads, so that people know we are doing something worthwhile. Thank you.

Chris Wood
The Power of Magick Publishing

www.thepowerofmagick.com

Other books from The Power of Magick

Angelic Sigils, Seals and Calls
Ben Woodcroft

Discover 142 Angels and Archangels, and the secret sigils, keys and calls that let you make instant contact with them.

Angelic Protection Magick
Ben Woodcroft

Angelic protection is gentle, calm and kind, yet powerful, subtle and cunning. This bright, white magick can make your enemies tremble with awe while keeping you safe with the power of light.

7 Occult Money Rituals
Henry Archer

This book contains simple rituals that bring the money you desire. No demons, no darkness. You get powerful, light magick, using angelic names and sigils. Your wants and needs are converted into reality, through the power of magick.

The Magick of Angels and Demons
Henry Archer

Combine the magick of angels and demons and you get an unheard-of way to control your life. The Union of Power is a priceless method for tasking the angels and demons, without any sacrifice or lengthy rituals.

Lucifer and The Hidden Demons
Theodore Rose

There are more than 100 demons in this book, and most are unknown outside of the secret orders. You will have the ability to work with hundreds of unique powers.

Printed in Poland
by Amazon Fulfillment
Poland Sp. z o.o., Wrocław